MW01699979

I began working with Bethany Mooradian almost 10 years ago, when she contacted my company about becoming a secret shopper. Little did I know at the time, that Bethany was not "just a shopper," but an entrepreneur extraordinaire with an extremely high standard of excellence. In all of her endeavors, Bethany seeks to support and serve others, while making the best of every situation she encounters. Even under fire, Bethany maintains her composure, grace, enthusiasm and incredible sense of humor. In reading "Become a Mystery Shopper!" you will gain great insight into what it takes to be a sensational secret shopper. You will also have fun while you learn, as you experience through Bethany's eyes what secret shopping is REALLY like. She has a humorous, engaging writing style, while providing accurate and practical information. This book will hold your attention, and you will refer back to it again and again throughout your mystery shopping career!

—Joyce Kirby, owner Shoptalk Service Evaluations (**www.shoptalkservice.com**)

Bethany is a good friend and mentor for me and my husband. Her wealth of knowledge and advice is drawn from her wide range of life experiences and business pursuits. She has a bounty to offer anyone from any walk of life. I have used her mystery shopping CD-ROM and materials to jumpstart my own mystery shopping pursuits, and the materials are not only clear and easy to follow but also humorous and entertaining. She presents the information sequentially and points out the possible pitfalls and scams to look for in the realm of mystery shopping. And the advice does not stop there - at any point, contact Bethany with any questions or concerns, and she will get back to you! This woman is successful, savvy, and most of all, sweet!

—Christine Kaputsky-Moore, Ian Tadashi-Moore (**www.iantm.com)**

I ordered Bethany Mooradian's Mystery Shopping Training Program a few months ago and it was the best investment I could have made. Bethany explains in detail how to get assignments, how write a report, and provides a list of legitimate companies to work for. Bethany's training program book is my bible! She is always there long after me buying the program to help and answer any questions I have. Mystery shopping is a great part time job and Bethany did an excellent job creating this training program. I highly recommend it!

—DS in Michigan

When I was looking to supplement my income, I turned to Bethany's "Become a Mystery Shopper" program. Within days I was accepting and completing assignments like a pro. The information she provided was clear, concise, and really helped me avoid the pitfalls and scams. Bethany has also been an invaluable resource in helping me streamline my business practices. Her knowledge of all things Internet has propelled me to a level of success I never knew possible! Any time I have questions regarding scams, marketing and social media, she is the first on my list to contact. Actually, she is the only person I would trust in giving me the whole picture about home based jobs, Internet marketing, social media practices, and scams.
—Jen Davidson (Jen Davidson Photography)

Bethany is truly the most knowledgeable person I know. When I needed extra money while trying to start my business, she taught me creative ways to earn an income. I continue to e-mail her new opportunities I see on Craigslist, and she always knows which ones are legit and which ones are scams. Her breadth of knowledge does not stop there, she also helps my new business with social media and keeps me updated on the newest Twitter rules and standards and ways to pimp out my Facebook fan page! She is truly a maven and a godsend to my business.
—Shalonne Foster (**www.seattlefashiontv.com**)

Bethany is extremely knowledgeable about mystery shopping and similar employment opportunities. Her presentation was enthusiastic and realistic. I especially appreciated the book she provided with listings of real companies to get started with. She obviously enjoys sharing her experience and knowledge, and anyone would benefit from her classes.
—Anonymous student review through Canton Adult Education

Bethany makes working from home and Mystery Shopping sound like a real adventure! Her energy and enthusiasm throughout our class was contagious. I was really impressed with the book provided. It was comprehensive and laid out in a very organized manner. The class was well worth its value, and had much more information than I was expecting.
—Anonymous student review from Farmington Community Education

I really enjoyed Bethany's presentation! The information was comprehensive, well organized and thought out. Bethany was easy to follow and constantly asked if we had questions, making sure we all understood each concept before moving onto the next subject. She was amazingly knowledgeable and gave us numerous resources to pursue after class. I am highly impressed with her professionalism and was amazed that an adult education class could be so outstanding. She belongs on the lecture circuit!
—Anonymous student review through Dearborn Adult Education

Bethany exceeded my expectations and gave me all the information I wanted and more. I took both her mystery shopping and work from home classes and feel totally prepared to get started. The information she provided about scams alone was worth the price of admission! She was clear, concise, enthusiastic, engaging, personable, professional, and was genuine in her interaction. The books she provided were well organized, and I can't wait to get started!
—Anonymous student review through Shoreline Community College

Bethany did a fabulous job of introducing us to mystery shopping! I had no idea it could be so involved and so much FUN. I can hardly wait to get started. Her genuine enthusiasm and knowledge of the subject was contagious. I look forward to learning more about other ways to make extra income in the future.
—Anonymous student review through Troy Continuing Education

I recently was laid off from GM, and started cleaning out the house, looking for things to sell. I stumbled upon your Mystery Shopping program that I purchased a few years ago. The information was so easy to read, and well laid out, that I could just jump right into Mystery Shopping without hesitation. I knew where to get started, and what to avoid. Although I haven't been able to replace my income as a machinist, (I wasn't really expecting to) Mystery Shopping has gotten me through these hard times, helped me to feed my kids and give me a bit of hope. I know you probably don't remember me, but I wanted you to know that I remember you, and I'm so thankful that you took the time to help people like me find a way to make some extra money.
—Anonymous student from Royal Oak Community Education

THE MYSTERY SHOPPER TRAINING PROGRAM

Everything You Need Know
about the *BEST* Part-Time Job!

Bethany Mooradian

Moreradiant Publishing

The Mystery Shopper Training Program
Copyright © 2003, 2007, 2009, 2011 by Bethany Mooradian

Previously published as "The Become a Mystery Shopper Training Program" and "Shop Incognito's Become a Mystery Shopper Training Program"

All rights reserved. No part of this publication may be reproduced, distributed, or transmitted in any form or by any means, electronic or mechanical, including photocopying, recording, or by any information storage and retrieval system, without prior written permission from the publisher and author, except for brief quotations embodied in critical reviews and certain other noncommercial uses permitted by copyright law. For permission questions, write to the publisher.

All logos and trademarks are property of their respective companies.

This publication is designed to provide accurate and authoritative information with regard to the subject matter covered. It is sold with the understanding that the publisher is not engaged in rendering legal, accounting, or other professional advice. If legal advice or other expert assistance is required, the services of a competent professional person should be sought.
—From a Declaration of Principles jointly adopted by a Committee of the American Bar Association and a Committee of Publishers and Associations

ISBN13: 978-0-9802296-0-8
ISBN10: 098022960X
Published by Moreradiant Publishing
Printed in the United States of America

Contents

RESOURCES

FORMS

Introduction

I first learned about Mystery Shopping in 1999. At the time, I had just gotten off a year-long tour as a professional puppeteer and was looking for my next adventure. I found a book about odd jobs in hopes of supplementing my meager, random income. The book didn't give a lot of information about mystery shopping, just to contact local market research companies for information. I dutifully went through the yellow pages, and the very first company I called left me skeptical.

"Do you do…mystery shopping?" I tentatively asked.

"Why yes! Of course we do," said the woman, much like a used car salesman. "All you have to do is pay $40 to take our class, and YOU can become a mystery shopper!"

Right away, I was sure I was going to be scammed, and I HATE being scammed. I will admit that when I was in college, I did send away $19.95 so that I could learn how to become a millionaire stuffing envelopes at home. Surprisingly, that didn't work out, so I'm always hypersensitive about these "work from home" jobs. I signed up for the class anyway, and I actually was planning on canceling later on. After all, $40 is a lot of money to a broke puppeteer. The very next week, I got a frantic call.

"We have an EMERGENCY SHOP!" the woman said frantically (yes, there is such a thing as an "emergency shop"). "Someone was supposed to shop an apartment building, and they canceled, and we need it done and back into the client's hands by 5 P.M. TODAY! Can you do it?!?!?!"

I was horrified. I still didn't even understand what the heck mystery shopping was, and here they wanted me to go out into the real world and DO it?

"Um, ah, but I haven't even taken your class yet!" I mumbled.

"It's okay," said my contact, "Have you ever looked for an apartment before?"

I thought, *Of course!* We all have at some point looked for apartments, rooms for rent, new homes, something like that.

"That's all you have to do. Call the property, talk to a leasing agent over the phone, go to the apartment, evaluate the conditions of the apartment, the conditions of the community, the agent's closing style, and write up the report."

I was still uncertain, but she then e-mailed me a copy of the form, so that I knew exactly what to look for. I headed out to this $2,000-a-month luxury apartment community, all the time thinking, "I'm going to get caught. I have no business being in a $2,000-a-month apartment. I'm a puppeteer!"

But I didn't get caught. Somehow I managed to pull through, finish the shop and convince the leasing agent I actually fit in there. Two weeks later, I got my first check as a Mystery Shopper.

I've been shopping ever since!

Over the past 10-plus years, I have done every aspect of this business. I started out as a shopper, I've done scheduling and editing, I've worked with companies to train their employees, I've worked with mystery shopping companies to train their shoppers, I teach classes on mystery shopping, I wrote this book, I created the training CD, I co-created a scheduling software for shoppers, and for two years, I ran Shop Incognito, a full service mystery shopping company in the Detroit metropolitan area.

The great thing about mystery shopping is that it can be done anytime, anywhere. You are your own boss. You choose what assignments you want to take and when you want to complete them. I personally have shopped in nine different states and two different provinces. When I get burned out, I take a break. When

I'm ready to work again, I jump right back in. Mystery shopping is always available as a source of income.

Every business that deals with customers can be shopped: Apartments, banks, retail stores, self-storage facilities, cell phone providers, airlines, hotels, motels, and resorts, restaurants, bowling alleys, casinos, amusement parks, child-care providers, weight-loss facilities, and many more *all* have shopping programs. Shops are conducted in the United States, Canada, and around the world. There are even a host of professional organizations, conferences, trade shows, and certification courses for shoppers and companies to be involved in. Mystery shopping is a *real* business where you can make a great extra income!

My purpose with this program is to help you get started in the wonderful world of mystery shopping. I am going to walk you through every aspect of the business, and answer the questions you didn't even know you had.

In the U.S. and Canada, there are about 500 mystery shopping companies and I have listed over 170 in the Resource section to get you started. The ones I have selected have a good reputation within the industry, and they are ones that I, or my fellow shoppers, have worked for, so I can personally recommend them. If you exhaust this listing (in which case, I'd be really impressed!), I have also listed the professional organizations, message boards, and many more ways to find assignments and other companies to work for.

I can't guarantee that you'll find employment with the companies in this book. You need to develop the skills needed and conduct yourself in a professional manner to get assignments. By the time you finish this program, however, you'll definitely, be well versed on how to behave as a responsible, reliable shopper.

Good luck, and happy shopping!

Before You Begin!

This book was created as a reference for *The Mystery Shopper Training Program* CD Rom. If you do not have the video to guide you, please start by reading the Glossary before beginning the book so that you will at least be familiar with common terms within the mystery shopping industry.

If you were sold this book without a video, it may be a pirated or used copy. However, you can still purchase a video if you so choose through **www.QueenoftheRandomJob.com**. It's up to you whether you want to return to the point of purchase, grumble at the owner, and try and get the full program. It would probably be quicker and easier (and more cost-effective) just to get the video directly from **www.QueenoftheRandomJob.com**, but again, it's your choice!

Chapter 1

What Is Mystery Shopping?

Mystery shopping is an aspect of market research. I'm sure you've heard of "focus groups" where people sit around a table to talk about the kind of kitty litter that they buy so the company can make it "new and improved." That's market research. Mystery shopping is just another way to get a customer's opinion.

Have you ever had a great experience at a store? One where the employee really went the extra mile for you? Conversely, have you ever had an experience where an employee just didn't get it? Very rarely do patrons of a store actually contact the management to praise or complain about employees or services. As customers, we are more likely to tell our *friends and families* about an experience at a store rather than the management. Mystery shopping is a tool that companies use to get inside a customer's head, so that they can improve their business.

As a mystery shopper, you will be asked to report back on how employees, products, and services are viewed by the average person. The companies can use this information to:

- Evaluate customer service
- Observe loss prevention methods
- Maintain compliance issues (alcohol and tobacco purchases)
- Observe fair housing practices

- Train employees on proper and improper methods of interacting with a customer
- Improve the cleanliness, surroundings, products, and services
- Motivate employees with bonuses, rewards, and incentives
- Observe potential employees
- Observe the competition within their industry

Any one of these reasons can help a business to build better customer service, employee satisfaction, and improve productivity within the workplace.

Mystery shopping was first developed as a way to check on employees and their honesty. Creating "integrity" evaluations, people would pose as customers to make sure that the employee was doing everything as he or she should: closing a cash drawer, ringing the proper sale amount, giving back correct change, etc. These evaluations helped with a company's loss-prevention program. With the influx of security cameras, point-check stands and other technological advances, mystery shopping evolved into a customer service evaluation program.

The most common misconception about mystery shopping is that shoppers are hired to get employees fired. This couldn't be further from the truth. Mystery shoppers are hired to see what a company is doing right, and how it can improve. As a mystery shopper, you will be asked to give an honest and objective evaluation about the service you received. Simple as that!

Although it does sound too good to be true, mystery shopping is a legitimate way to earn a great part-time income. There are professional organizations, certification courses, Web forums, and conventions devoted to the practice of mystery shopping.

As a mystery shopper, you get to choose what kind of assignments you want to accept, be it a restaurant, movie theater, retail store, self-storage facility, bank, grocery store, apartment community, or whatever else piques your interest. You set your schedule depending on your availability and what cities you want to shop in. You can shop in the mornings, afternoons, evenings, weekends, on your lunch break, or even when you're on vacation! There are shops all over the world just waiting to be accepted. You do not have to have any experience to get started (if you live in Nevada or Texas, check around, because you may need to get a private investigator's license), just the ability to take notice of details, be objective in your opinions, and write clear narratives of your experience.

How It Works

Mystery shopping companies, *not the individual stores*, hire shoppers. Do not call your local grocery store, retail outlet, or bank and ask about mystery shopping. The employees can't help you, and you run the risk of giving yourself away as a shopper before you get started!

Mystery shopping can be viewed as a 3-tiered system:

The "**Client**" (Department Stores, Chain Restaurants, etc.)
hires the
Mystery shopping company, (ABC Shoppers)
which then in turn hires the
Mystery shopper (YOU!)

It is imperative that you remain anonymous as a mystery shopper. That's where the middleman, the mystery shopping company, comes in. It will contract you as a mystery shopper. It will talk to the stores, the apartment buildings and the service providers, to set up shops to be completed by you, the shopper. That way the people at the stores you visit will never know who you are. This way, you don't have to worry about some disgruntled employee knocking on your door at three o'clock in the morning!

Clients used to have their own shopping programs, but then all of the owners, managers, and eventually employees got to know the mystery shopper. It's hard to have an objective evaluation when everybody knows who the shopper is!

Shops are found in several different ways:

1. The mystery shopping company will place available assignments on its own or other websites and hope that shoppers will fill them on their own. This is the quickest way to get assignments, as you don't have to wait for schedulers to contact you. You can pick and choose what assignments you want from those available.

2. It has people within the company who schedule shops to shoppers, either through individual contact or mass e-mailings. Some companies are now set up on Twitter and Facebook and post available assignments there as well.

3. For whatever reason, the mystery shopping company is too big, too small, or too busy, so it hires independent scheduling companies to take care of assigning and editing shops.

Mystery shopping companies range in size. They can be very large with hundreds of employees, offering other services in addition to mystery shopping. The benefit of working with a large company is that you can be considered for a greater number of assignments. You also have the benefit of being one of many, so you won't be called every second for a job, since there are other shoppers who can fill assignments.

Some companies consist of just a handful of people. The benefit of working with smaller companies is that they tend to provide better service to the shopper and the business being shopped. If you provide quality work, you are more likely to get preferential assignments. You tend to develop closer relationships with smaller companies, and you will receive assistance unlike that which you get from a larger, multifaceted corporation.

Chapter 2

FAQ about Mystery Shopping Companies

How is a Mystery Shopping Company Different From a Scheduling Company?

Mystery shopping companies have clients that need their businesses shopped. They develop the forms and handle the payroll of their shoppers. Some mystery shopping companies will handle all of the scheduling and editing of the forms that are submitted with in-house schedulers. Others prefer to outsource that work to individual schedulers or scheduling companies.

Scheduling companies deal with recruiting shoppers, filling available assignments, scheduling assignments, and sometimes editing the form and soliciting follow-up information from the shopper. They are not responsible for paying the shopper or finding the clients. This allows mystery shopping companies to focus on their business, and it allows scheduling companies to work with a variety of mystery shopping companies for a broad range of assignments.

As a mystery shopper, you want to sign on with both the individual mystery shopping companies and the scheduling companies. Since scheduling companies work with several mystery shopping companies, you'll receive many more job offers!

What Do Companies Need to Know About Me?

When filling out an application, be prepared to give demographic information that usually isn't requested in other lines of work. Your income, ethnic heritage, age, and so on may be optional to disclose, but employers need to know this information to see if you qualify for a shop. Generally, a company would not ask an 18 year-old to go into a bank and ask for a home equity loan. Likewise, they're not going to send my 94 year-old grandmother into a nightclub. No matter how hip she is, she doesn't fit the profile!

Sometimes people of ethnic background are needed to test the "fair housing laws" of an apartment community. Some companies request that you submit a photo of yourself. Don't be concerned that this information will prevent you from receiving assignments. The majority of work is available regardless of age or income or the type of car you drive. Providing this extra information will give you more opportunities for specialty shops when the client is looking for a specific type of person (for example, when a mother of young children is needed to check out a day care center).

How Often Will I Be Contacted for Work?

Shops will be assigned in your area as they become available. They won't be available until a business hires a mystery shopping company to have shops performed. Some businesses order random shops when needed, others are set up on a schedule where they're shopped every month or quarter. It's all very relative.

What About Mystery Shopping Companies Located Out of My Local Area?

It is generally assumed that companies work in their local area. Some may branch out to different states, provinces, and countries.

There could be a mystery shopping company that specializes in covering the New England area but also has one major client located in Texas. The areas where shops occur constantly change for companies, so it is recommended that you sign up for a company, even if it isn't currently doing shops in your area. A few months from now, they may need someone in your area, and you might be its only hope! However, if it is specifically noted on the application that it doesn't need shoppers in your area, don't apply. Don't bug your schedulers to see when they'll have assignments in your area. They'll contact you when you're needed.

How Can I Request Shops?

Depending on the mystery shopping company, you can expect to receive e-mail about upcoming work, or you can expect to frequent a website to find available shops. Some are set up for Facebook and Twitter, and broadcast their available assignments in addition to posting on job boards and sending e-mails.

You might want to set up an independent e-mail account reserved for just shopping. Don't worry about spam. Mystery shopping companies will NOT sell your information. In the past decade, I've signed up with over 150 companies. I have never received ONE piece of spam in my mystery shopping e-mail account. It's a free account, and you'd think I'd get spam just because it exists, but it hasn't happened and I am very thankful!

When deadlines get tight, some companies will contact shoppers by phone to fill available shops. Some companies prefer that you submit a "bid" to request a shop. This means that you will receive a list of available shops for an upcoming month, and you enter your name for a particular date range of completing assignments. The scheduler draws up a schedule, and you receive information on the shops that have been assigned to you.

What Happens When I Receive a Job Offer?

You'll receive a mass e-mail notice of an available assignment in your area. The company will tell you when the assignment needs to be done, sometimes being very specific, "Between 5-8 p.m. on Friday, January 31" or vague, stating that the shop must be completed "within the next month." In that case, you get to pick when you'd like to complete the assignment. They will tell you the type of assignment, where it is located, and the rate of pay. They will NOT tell you the specific client's name, because they want to protect the identity of the client and stipulations of the assignment until is it actually assigned.

Once you have accepted an assignment, the company is responsible for providing current, accurate, detailed information about the shop. You should be given the name of the business you are shopping, the name of the target (if there is a specific employee to evaluate), date or time-frame for the shop to be completed, the date that the shop is due back to the company, possible scenarios or cover stories, location of the business, and your scheduler's phone number should a problem arise. If you have a target, see if you can get your target's schedule, so that you can arrive at an appropriate time. The company will give you detailed instructions including what needs to be done in order to get paid, (for example, getting an associate's name) and expenses that they might cover like mileage, postage, purchases, or parking.

Here is an example of a mass e-mail to fill an assignment.

*** June Bank Shops Available ***

Mystery shoppers are needed in the NEW YORK cities listed below for BANK SHOPS. Payment is $20 and requires an inquiry for a new checking or savings account. Shops may NOT be done on Saturday, or after 5 p.m. Assignments are due before June 26. An online report will need to be completed with detailed comments regarding your experience.

Manhattan New York City Westfield Rochester

If interested, YOU MUST FIRST sign up on our website at www.fictionalwebsite.com to become a shopper, if you have not done so already. After registering, complete the information below and e-mail to: shops@fictionalwebsite.com

**** List locations desired in e-mail Subject Line ****
Name:
Phone:
E-mail:
List ALL location's desired in order of preference:
When could you complete this shop?

Further details will be sent upon receiving the assignment.

Before performing a shop, some companies will make you take a brief training on the type of shop you will be performing, so that you are familiar with the questions that need to be answered. Sometimes you are required to go through this training during the application process.

Depending on the company, you will submit your write-up either by fax, mail, or over the Web. When possible, make a copy of the shop for your records. If the evaluation form is sent via the Internet, you should receive some sort of confirmation, such as a tracking number or an acknowledgement from a representative. Do NOT wait around to receive a confirmation! Be pro-active in making sure that the company has received your work. If your report gets lost in the depths of the Internet, or in the mail, or over the fax lines, you *will not be paid!*

How Will I Get Paid?

Payment timeframes vary by company. The general rule of thumb is that you should expect to be paid no later than the month after the month you complete the assignment.

For example, if a shop is completed in January, expect to be paid by the end of February. Some companies use PayPal or direct deposit instead of sending checks. In general, you'll get a much quicker turn around with these forms of payment (usually within 7 to 14 days). It really depends on the company, and that's why it is so important to keep track of your business. Since your income will be sporadic, make sure to keep track of all the companies you work for so that you don't forget about an overdue payment.

Also keep in mind that if you make over $599 in a calendar year from any one company, you should receive a 1099 form to report your taxes. We'll discuss the joy of taxes in the next chapter.

Chapter 3

Expectations and Responsibilities of Shoppers

Accepting Shops

Before you accept ANY shop, be sure that you can DO the shop within the allowed time and that you understand the guidelines, pay schedule, and requirements. Make sure that you WANT to do the assignment. Remember, you don't have to accept a shop for fear that a company may not hire you again. This is the most flexible job you will ever have. If you want to take two months off, do so. If you're traveling and want to pick up shops along the way, go for it! Companies will not judge you on the number of shops you complete; they care about the quality of work provided. That is the key to getting repeat assignments and consideration for more exclusive shops. Remember, when you get those mass e-mails, you'll receive enough information about the assignment to decide whether or not you want to commit to it.

Returning Correspondence

If you have e-mail, you will get mass correspondence from schedulers or mystery shopping companies looking for people to fill jobs. When you receive e-mails from schedulers, it is important to note that, in most cases, you do not need to reply unless you want the job. It can get frustrating for schedulers who send out offers of upcoming assignments to receive e-mails back that say nothing more than, "Thanks, but no thanks," from the majority of people on their e-mail list. If you want the assignment, reply. If not, let it be. The schedulers will appreciate you for it!

If you want an assignment that is offered to you, make sure to reply in the manner requested. They're going to tell you how they want you to apply: this is a weeding-out process!

There is a high "flake factor" in mystery shopping. There are a lot of people who think this is just something fun and don't take the work seriously. A lot of times shoppers will drop assignments or simply not follow directions! The scheduler is going to tell you "put your name on the first line, put the cities you want to shop on the second line" and so on, to see if you can follow directions. DO NOT just reply asking for more information. They already have given everything that they can tell you in their e-mail. Do exactly what is asked of you, and you'll be sure to receive more and more assignments.

Returning Shops

Life happens. Sometimes things come up and you cannot complete a shop as you had planned. Maybe your child is really sick, your car broke down, or there is really inclement weather. Whatever the case, be sure to contact the company IMMEDIATELY upon realizing that you cannot do the shop. It has a schedule to keep, and is relying on you to do your work. Do NOT just ignore the shop and figure that the company won't notice. It will. These last minute "emergency shops" sometimes pay a little more due to the need of getting them completed quickly. (Sometimes they pay a bonus as well!) If you forget to do the shop entirely, expect that the mystery shopping company won't call you again. Mystery shopping is a small industry. Everyone knows that you will be working for other companies and chances are that they know people at those companies as well. It is very easy to develop a reputation…be it good or bad.

Keeping Confidences

When you sign with a company, you will need to sign an Independent Contractor Agreement (ICA). This agreement varies with each company but generally means that you are responsible for your own taxes, you are not an employee of the company, and most importantly that you cannot reveal to *anyone* what you learn during your shop, or the clients of companies. In simpler terms, you can't reveal, "Who Shops Who."

This can be tricky, because in a lot of employment applications companies want to know other companies you have worked for.

It is not a violation of your agreement to list the names of the companies who have hired you. In your application, you could say that you have worked for "ABC Shoppers" but could not say that you have performed shops for "Billy Bob's House of Pancakes, through ABC Shoppers." Some companies ask you to offer this information just to see if you will break your agreements with other companies! It is easier to avoid the whole mess by offering samples of your work or references. Being a mystery shopper means that your identity *must* remain anonymous, and you have to demonstrate respect for the ICA in order to continue receiving work.

Making a Living

Mystery shopping is a job, it is in no way a get-rich-quick income. It is a unique way to earn an extra income without *feeling* like you are actually working. The appeal of mystery shopping is that it suits many types of people who don't have the schedule, time, or desire for a typical nine-to-five job. Students, stay-at-home moms, artists, retirees, and those wanting a second income have benefited from this flexible part-time opportunity.

Shops are generally given a set price for completion. You can expect to make an average of about $15 on retail shops, $35 on apartment shops, and general reimbursement for entertainment and restaurant shops. All in all, including shop time, travel, and filling out the form, you can expect to average between $10-$25 per hour. However, the closer a shop gets to a deadline, the more paranoid a company gets that it won't be filled. In these cases bonuses are sometimes offered, so don't be afraid to ask for more money! Especially if it's out of your normal travel route and you need a little extra for gas or to compensate for the extra travel time. You are an independent contractor, and there is nothing wrong with bargaining to get the best rate for your services. Doing it all the time, however, might tarnish your reputation, and it isn't recommended for a company where you don't have a history. If you can do a good job, but just need a little extra to make it worth your while, there is no reason why you can't be compensated for it.

What about Taxes?

I am not a tax professional, and you should contact a reliable tax attorney to assist you with your taxes. What I know is based on my own experiences, and your situation may be different, so please take that into consideration when reading through this section.

As a mystery shopper, you will be considered an independent contractor. The Mystery Shopping companies will not withhold taxes from your checks; you are responsible for that. The plus side to running your own business is that you do get to deduct everything related to your business and usually end up paying only Social Security.

When I say deduct *everything*, I mean the mileage on your car, your Internet access, the ink cartridges and paper for your printer, your cell phone, clip-board, disks or thumb drives, faxes, classes that you had to take, instructional materials (this program!) training, and so on. It is important to keep track of everything to make tax time easier.

The bad news is that since you aren't an employee, you are not eligible for insurance, unemployment, Workers Compensation, or benefits. Some companies go so far as to say in your contractual agreement that if you get into an accident at your shopping location, you cannot hold the shopping company responsible. Make sure that you read those agreements carefully before you sign them! You should also make sure that you can either deduct or save around 30% of your income: that's what dear ol' Uncle Sam wants from those who are self-employed. Remember that if you have earned more than $599 in a calendar year from a company, it is required to send you a 1099 form so that you can report your income.

If You're Moving

Mystery shopping is conducted all over the world, so no matter where you live, there is a possibility of working as a mystery shopper! If you do move, make sure that you contact all the companies that you are registered with to update your contact information. When you sign up with companies, they are going to ask for the area codes, ZIP codes, or specific cities you in which you want to shop. If you start shopping in Boston, and then move to San Francisco, the company needs to know!

Shopping on Vacation

If you want to pick up some shopping assignments while you're on vacation, first contact the companies you work with to find out if they do shopping in that area. Many have websites where you can search for assignments in various area codes, so you may not actually have to talk to someone directly.

Another approach is to go to the Mystery Shopping Providers Association (MSPA) website, or other job board websites, and click through to the city and state where you'll be vacationing. You'll see listings of available shops, and the companies that perform them. If you're not already signed up with them, go ahead and register.

The trickiest part about shopping on vacation is finding a Internet access to submit your report. If you're visiting relatives, or friends who have computers and the Internet, (or bring your own laptop) you'll be pretty much set. Most hotels have Wi-Fi access, or a business center where you can get online. Outside of these options, find a cyber café, or use the local library. They library is usually free and you can check e-mails, submit reports, and keep up to date with your shopping business. The nice thing about shopping on your vacation is that you can deduct part of your trip as a business expense.

Chapter 4

Keeping Track of Your Business

It is imperative that you keep track of the companies you shop for and the shops that you perform. Do *not* expect the companies to remember what you did last week, last month, or last year. This is *your* responsibility.

Also, remember that the shopping companies are only made up of people who are human. Your shop could have gotten lost. If you don't have a confirmation from the shopping company, *you won't get paid*! If you forget to mail, fax, or scan a receipt from a purchase, *you won't get reimbursed*. If you accept a shop that you did last month, and someone overlooked the fact that you can only do it every OTHER month, *you won't get paid*!

Think of being a mystery shopper as running your own business. It is up to *you* to make sure that everything is accounted for. It is very important to keep receipts and a copy of any shop that you perform *at least* until you get paid. Some companies request that you keep a copy of the shops for 90 days or longer.

When you shop for more than one company, you need to be very organized. At the very least, you need a spreadsheet to account for the company, the assignment, pay rate, etc. On the next page is a sample that you can use as a template.

Business	Target	Amt	Due	Done	Expense	Paid	Company	Scheduler	Confirm
Shady Pines Apts	Connie	$30	1/15	1/13	15 miles	1/31	Apartments R Us	Giovanni	yes
Copier Central	None	$15	1/15	1/14	$5 fax, 3 miles	2/15	Shop for Fun	Computer	X52 SU9
Vic's Bowl-a-Rama	None	$5	1/21	1/21	$25 to reimburse	2/15	Shop for Fun	Computer	F7J MN8
Mo' Money Banks	None	$20	1/21	1/13	5 miles	2/28	Telus Incorporate	Jake	Yes

Let's examine the spreadsheet. Take a look at Shady Pines Apartments. Here you have a target: Connie. You want to remember that you talked to Connie, because should you do another shop at Shady Pines Apartments, you probably want to do it when Connie isn't there. To preserve anonymity, it is best that you don't visit the same retail location within a 3-4 month period; or an apartment community within a 6-month period.

The amount that you were paid for the shop was $30. It was due on January 15, but because you were such a good shopper you completed it on January 13. Your expense for the shop was just mileage.

Obviously, if you were going to a restaurant, you'd have food to put in this column, but even if you really liked the apartment, and decided to rent it, I don't think its tax deductible. All you can deduct is the 15 miles you traveled for the assignment. The day you were paid by the company was January 31 (quick turn-around!) and the company you worked for was Apartments R Us.

It's good to note that your scheduler was Giavonni, because if there are any questions, you know who to talk to. Make sure that you have a confirmation, something that states your work was received.

Looking at Vic's Bowl-a-Rama, you'll see that you obviously don't have a target, and that the payment for the assignment was just **$5**. That doesn't seem like much, but, if you look over in the expense column, it says, $25 to reimburse. What this means is that the company said, "We'll give you $5 for filling out the form, and $25 to go bowling with. Buy some frames, each some nachos, have a good time. We'll reimburse you up to $25."

When the company states it will reimburse you "up to" a certain amount, remember that that's your limit. If you spend $26.50, you'll get reimbursed $25. If you spend $21.37, you'll get reimbursed $21.37. The company will reimburse you up to the amount stated. In terms of taxes, the only money that you need to worry about declaring is the $5. Since you are being reimbursed for your bowling and nachos, that money is not considered income. In essence, you get a free night out!

In the "confirmation" column, there's a sort of cryptic number: F7J MN8. This means that the report was submitted online at the company's website. When you hit "submit report" you receive a random number. **Be sure to write it down**. You never know what happens over the Internet, and if your report gets lost and you can't prove you sent it, you won't be paid. You can also save the form as a text document in Word (some companies request this) just in case.

One of the downsides about mystery shopping is that you do need to apply to each company individually. You can save some time with this laborious process by applying to scheduling companies, letting mystery shopping companies share your information with other mystery shopping companies (on some websites you can check a box for this free service,) or signing up to be in a database that schedulers will mass e-mail. There are also businesses that, for a fee, will allow you to fill out one application form and submit to several mystery shopping companies at once. With a little extra time and effort however, you can save yourself the fees associated with any of these services.

There are hundreds of mystery shopping companies that service the U.S. and Canada. I personally am signed up with more than 150 of them, and that's a lot of information to keep track of! In the company listing section of this book, you'll have a place to keep track of your user IDs and passwords. You can create a spreadsheet to log your assignments, or work with a program like Microsoft Outlook™.

After years of shopping, I got really tired of all the paperwork associated with keeping track of my assignments, so I enlisted the help of software developer, and together we created TRIBEStrack™.

Originally created for Mystery Shoppers, this is a comprehensive solution that allows any independent contractor to keep track of their work. You'll be able to create company profiles, schedule your assignments, run reports for tax purposes and so much more. It's a combination of a digital calendar, client rolodex, GPS system, and accounting software all in one.

For more information you can visit my website: **www.QueenoftheRandomJob.com** or **www.TRIBEStrack.com.**

Chapter 5

Tools of the Trade

As with any profession, there are certain tools that you will need to be a successful mystery shopper. I highly recommend getting a computer, Internet access, and a tape recorder. Other things are optional, but definitely useful, when you are out on assignments. Remember, should you spend any money on your mystery shopping business, it could be tax deductible so save your receipt!

Personality Traits

To be a successful mystery shopper, you need certain physical and mental abilities. Your assignments will require you to demonstrate good memory, observation skills, flexibility, accuracy, honesty, and reliability. You need to be computer proficient, with a basic understanding of the Internet, e-mail, spreadsheets, and word-processing programs. Since you are in charge of your own business, and responsible for submitting timely information to companies, you will need to be organized, thorough, and detail-oriented. It always helps to have a friendly personality, and the willingness to help your scheduler out when they need to get assignments filled.

Technology

With technology advancing so quickly, it is rare to find assignments that do not require a computer or Internet access. A few companies still work with pen and paper, but these shops require more advance notice, as the company will need to send the forms to you by regular mail. You need to make sure that your handwriting is legible, unless you still own a typewriter, in which case, be sure to have plenty of white-out. If you do not have a computer or Internet access, many local libraries do. Usually library access is free if you have a card, or at least a nominal rate per hour.

E-mail

Most companies assign shops through the company web site, or by emailing their shoppers as assignments come up. Some companies also use forms that are sent as attachments. If you do not already have an e-mail account, you can get a free one through **www.gmail.com, www.yahoo.com** or **www.hotmail.com**. I do recommend that you set up a separate email account specifically for your mystery shopping business. That way, if you ever want to take a break, you don't have to unsubscribe from receiving assignments. If you are not very Web Savvy, a community education course, or one through your local library can help you to learn the basics.

Computer Programs

Two computer programs that are used frequently for company forms are Microsoft Word® and Microsoft Excel®. There are plenty of community classes to help people figure out how to use these programs; the shopping company should also be able to help you fill out its forms. Adobe® Acrobat Reader is also used for forms (you can download the program from **www.adobe.com)**. With some Adobe forms you can type information directly onto the form. With others, you have to print out the form and mail, fax or scan it back to the company.

Fax Machines

Fax machines will make your life easier, but they are not a requirement for mystery shopping. Sometimes companies need to fax you instructions, or you might need to fax your receipts. If you don't have or want a fax machine, a free service called Efax allows you to receive faxes as an attachment to your email. After you receive an out-of-state "fax" number, people can fax you a document at this number. You cannot send faxes with the free service, but for a monthly charge, you can try out the company's other services; visit **www.efax.com** for information. An alternative to faxing is to use a scanner and a photo program to send items over the Internet through e-mail. Check your scanner software for information on how to use this feature.

Phones

Cell and car phones are not an absolute necessity for mystery shopping but they really come in handy. At this point, most people have cell phones but in case you don't, remember that they're tax deductible! If you ever find yourself completely lost, get bad directions, or have to reset an appointment, your cell phone could be a life saver. Sometimes shops don't go as they are supposed to; let's say you were supposed to buy a particular item, but the store just ran out. Having immediate contact with a scheduler could really make the difference. Also, some companies require that you call them right after the shop to answer some quick questions, or confirm that it was completed.

If you don't have access to a cell phone, make sure that you have change with you for a pay phone. If you haven't noticed, pay phones are 50 cents now!

Cameras: Video and Digital

Sometimes digital cameras are required for shops. Companies like to get a true "picture" of the shopper's experience; with other types of market research, they can be used to see if an establishment is up to code. You may be asked to take photos of specific sales signage in a retail store, or a company may need to photograph a delivery pizza to make sure the anchovies haven't shifted during delivery. It is definitely not a requirement to have a camera, and you can perform many shops without one, but sometimes there is an added bonus for completing shops that need cameras.

Digital video shops are becoming increasing popular. You will be given a little camera to wear, either in a hat, tie, or as a brooch, as you go through the assignment. Very rarely are written reports needed for video shops! You will usually have to go through some additional training with the company and provide a valid driver's license to be considered for these assignments.

Tape Recorders

A tape recorder is an absolute MUST for every shopper to have. It is always easier to record information about a shop while it is still fresh in your mind. Do NOT take the tape recorder with you! Some states have laws against recording people's voices without their consent (unlike video shops) and if you get caught doing so, you could be sued. Leave the tape recorder and a printed copy of your assignment form in the car while you shop. Once you're finished, you can drive down the road so you're out of view of the location, pull over and then verbally fill out the form. That way, you'll be able to type out the assignment word for word so you won't have to rely on your memory. Just keep in mind to talk slowly!

Apartment Rental Guides and Craigslist

When doing apartment shops, it is always handy to know something about the community before you call. Free guides like *The Apartment Guide* and *For Rent,* can be picked up at a local grocery or drug store. These guides are nice because they give information about the apartment like price range, amenities, and directions. Nearly every apartment community uses Craigslist to advertise their vacancies. Just by searching for an apartment name or phone number in the apartment ads, you'll pull up all of that community's listings and get a good idea on price range and amenities.

The apartments advertised in the free guides are usually the ones who get shopped! Most "Ma/Pa" places don't have evaluations performed, unless it's for competition shops: to see what others in the area are doing. Some apartment guides provide shopping services for the apartments that advertise with them, so you'll actually be shopping those who are in the book! Because some apartment guides also have award ceremonies each year, you might be hired as a shopper to evaluate "Best Leasing Agent," "Best Property Supervisor," "Best Landscaping," "Best Phone Presentation," "Best Manager," and so on.

Stopwatch/Timer

If you enjoy restaurant shops, a stopwatch (or a watch with a second-hand) is definitely needed. Some fast food places have timing guidelines for how quickly their customers receive food. They want you in and out in less than five minutes. In finer dining restaurants, the owners want to know how long it took for you to be greeted, seated, to receive your food, drinks, and bill. It's imperative that you have a watch to keep track. When I say "stopwatch", I do NOT mean one of those huge sports watches. You're not racing your server in some sort of track meet! Use something small (on your wrist), that either counts the seconds or lets you stop and start the time. You do need to be subtle. If a waitress sees you timing her, you will definitely be spotted as a shopper.

Maps/GPS

A map is another necessity. No matter how long you have lived in an area, there is always a new way to get lost. You don't necessarily have to run out and spend $60 on a Thomas Guide (although those are SO nice) or drop a few hundred on a GPS system. Remember that there are maps in the front section of phone books, you can always use Google Maps (**www.maps.google.com**) Yahoo! Maps (**www.maps.yahoo.com**) or MapQuest (**www.mapquest.com**) to help plot your route. These websites are particularly helpful when you are doing more than one shop in a day, when you need to travel from one to the next, and to keep track of your mileage.

Social Media Accounts

Many mystery shopping companies have taken their business to the Web and post their assignments on Twitter (**www.twitter.com)** and Facebook (**www.facebook.com)**. If you have accounts at either of these sites, they'll help you get those last-minute and emergency shops. Remember to keep your posts professional. You don't want a company to read your complaints about a recent assignment!

TRIBEStrack™ or Accounting/Scheduling Software

As a mystery shopper, you're going to be working for more than one company and it is imperative that you keep good records for your business. TRIBEStrack™ is a software program I co-developed specifically with the independent contractor in mind. It will allow you to:

- Create company profiles with contact information
- Schedule Assignments
- Log payments
- Log deductions and mileage
- Run reports for tax and accounting purposes
- And more!

You can also use programs like Outlook™ and Quickbooks™, or create your own spreadsheet or filing system.

For more information on TRIBEStrack™ and to see how it can help you become more organized as a mystery shopper or independent contractor, visit **www.QueenoftheRandomJob.com** or **www.TRIBEStrack.com**.

Chapter 6

Not Quite Shopping

Some mystery shopping companies are specifically geared toward mystery shopping, while others branch out into other types of market research such as merchandising, audits, forums, mock trials, or surveying.

Merchandising

Have you ever gone into a store, saw someone stacking shelves, asked them for help and heard, "I don't work here?" Those people are called merchandisers. They're working in the store but are contracted by an outside organization to replace signage, restock shelves, and check the prices on cereal boxes. Depending on the assignment and company, merchandisers are paid per assignment or per hour. The average rate of pay will be around $10-$12 an hour, and some companies pay for mileage.

If you have the free time, and you need the money, it's nice to be able to pop into a place and work for a short time. Some assignments last for months, others are one-time only.

When you do merchandising, you will have contact with the employees and managers and are not considered a "mystery shopper." It is best that you don't identify yourself as a shopper, because someday you might actually be contracted to do a shop there. You can find this type of work through mystery shopping companies, merchandising companies, in the Help Wanted section of your local newspaper under "merchandisers" or "general help wanted", by searching "merchandising" on Craigslist job boards, and through a temp agency.

Audits

Audits can be one-time assignments, or monthly engagements to analyze a particular aspect of a store. These can range greatly, depending on what the company is looking for. Sometimes you'll be hired to go into a store to make sure that is has specific sale signage up. Remember the signage that the merchandiser put up? Sometimes an auditor will follow behind the merchandiser, to make sure they did it correctly. Other times you'll need to count the number of patrons in a movie theater during a particular weekend. Depending on the requirements, you may need to act as a shopper, and not give away your identity, or you may be requested to work with the management about your findings. Either way, audits are generally paid a one-time fee, not an hourly rate.

Forums and Focus Groups

Forums are what people generally think of when they hear "market research." This is when companies are trying to solicit the opinions of regular people about a particular product or service. These events vary greatly depending on what the company is trying to achieve.

Sometimes you will be shown a video and then asked for your opinion. You might be called in to taste-test different kinds of pizza or soft drinks. You might be asked to give your opinion on political campaign commercials or brochures. You might be given a product to use for a week or so and asked about what you thought of it.

Situations vary from open-forum discussion with a panel of other people to one-on-one in-depth discussions of your personal views.

You can find focus group work though your local market research companies. Many advertise on Craiglist under "etc", or you can search for "focus group" on the job boards to find listings. Before you give all of your personal information to the market research company, be sure to do some research of your own to make sure they're legitimate. Many scammers will pose as market research companies to find out your income, whether you own or rent, and other information to scam you! Do your due diligence: check out the company website, even visit their offices, to guarantee your own safety.

The pay for focus group work varies greatly, but generally pays really well for just 30-120 minutes of your time. I've seen them anywhere from $50 up to $250 and more.

Mock Trials

Mock trials are what they sound like: fabricated trials in which lawyers try out certain aspects of their case. You get to act as a juror and give feedback on the strength of their argument, their courtroom personality, and how the arguments sway you. Sometimes you'll be called in to hear a case when one side is trying to figure out if it needs to go to trial or should settle.

The time commitment varies with the case, and your compensation is generally a flat rate, depending on the company. You can get mock trail work through market research companies. You can also call a local law firm to see who it uses for mock trial scheduling and request to get on its list. If you dread jury duty though, this probably isn't for you.

Reward and Revealing Shops

Some mystery shoppers love these assignments, though others refuse to do them, as they require giving away your true identity! In a Reward/Revealing shop, the management wants to evaluate an aspect of service. That is to say, they want to see if an employee "up-sells" and will hire a mystery shopper to give a gift certificate, prize, or cash reward to an employee if the service is done correctly.

Let's say you go into a movie theater and ask, "Could I have the small, two-pound bag of popcorn please?" The employee replies, "Would you like to upgrade to the 'Mamajama' five-pound size for only $15 more?"

That's when you get to say, "Congratulations! I am a mystery shopper, and you correctly tried to up-sell me! You get this $20 gift certificate!"

The employee does a little happy dance, and all is right with the world.

These shops are fun, because more often than not, the employee does get rewarded, and it's nice to make people happy. Remember that you'll be giving yourself up as a shopper, so you'll want to stay away from that location for a few months. And yes, you'll still get to see the movie.

Surveying and Exit Interviewing

Have you ever seen those delightful people at the mall, clipboard in hand, asking everyone who even thinks about looking in their direction, "Would you like to take a survey?" You could be one of those people!

Some mystery shopping companies also participate in general market research surveys, called "exit interviews." As a researcher, you'll be placed in a mall, outside of a store or restaurant, ask people a few questions about the service they received and the products they bought. If you've ever been at the receiving end of one of these encounters, you know the respondent may get a gift certificate for their help or just a thankful smile. The surveyor may receive an hourly rate (generally about $10-12 per hour) or a flat fee for a certain number of hours, and sometimes a per-completed survey bonus.

Chapter 7

Types of Mystery Shops

The great thing about mystery shopping is that everyone gets shopped! No matter what you like to do, there are assignments to pique your interest. Below are some of the common types of shops you will see.

Phone

Financial institutions, real estate shops, automated call centers, catalogue orders, car rentals.

Rate: approximately $5-$15 depending on the form and company.

These can be the simplest shops to complete, taking only a few moments, with brief forms to fill out. Businesses know that it is important for their employees to conduct themselves in a professional manner over the phone, otherwise, the customer may not ever come into their establishment. When doing phone shops, it is important to note how long it took for the phone to be answered, if you were put on hold, if the associate was friendly and professional, and if he or she answered your questions and concerns in a confident manner.

You could be asked to call several businesses, or just one repeatedly over a period of weeks. It is important to learn how to be confidently anonymous. Feel free to give yourself a new name, address, and phone number, or just state that you prefer not to give out your contact information. You might get an assignment to call a business once a week for two months. It really helps if they don't know who you are, so Caller ID can be tricky. When you're doing a phone shop, dial *67 before the number: your phone number will show up as "Private number" on the Caller ID.

Web/Internet

Financial institutions, retail websites, real estate shops, automated call centers, catalogue orders, car rentals.

Rate: approximately $5-$40 depending on the form and company.

Now that most businesses are online, mystery shoppers are hired to evaluate how effective their online presence is. As a shopper you may be asked to fill out a "contact us" form to see how long an employee takes to respond to you with a quote or other information. You may be asked to go through the process of shopping online to rate your experience and how easy it was to use the site and shopping card.

Retail

Convenience stores, department, malls, outlet, discount stores.

Rate: approximately $5-$70, depending on the form and company. For some shops, you will be required to purchase an item as part of the evaluation. You may be asked to return the item to the store to get your money back (and evaluate the return process), you may be reimbursed by the mystery shopping company, or the purchase may count as part of your compensation.

Retail shops help businesses learn how quickly you were acknowledged, if the associate was friendly and helpful, if he or she was able to give suggestions based on your needs, if the products were displayed in a tasteful manner, and the check out procedures.

For the lower paying shops you might be asked to go into a store, spend about five minutes getting help with purchasing a gift, evaluate the cleanliness, and be on your way. Most retail shops pay in the $10-$25 range and require contact with a salesperson, as well as evaluation of the surroundings, cleanliness, sales technique, and check out procedures.

Department stores pay more because you evaluate more than one department. The forms are more involved only because they deal with more associates and scenarios. For these elaborate shops, a tape recorder is helpful; when you can leave each area after the shop you can accurately report your findings.

Restaurant

Restaurant, fast food, bar, coffeehouses, specialty.

Rate: approximately $5-$10 plus or already including reimbursement. For fine dining, you might receive gift certificates or receive reimbursement as payment (generally drinks, appetizers, dinner, and dessert for two).

These assignments used to be completed with gift certificates, but now are done mostly on a reimbursement basis. Gift certificates are no longer used because some shoppers took them and then failed to complete the assignment! Be sure you save your receipt so that you can get reimbursed for your meal.

Restaurants are all about timing: how long it took for you to be acknowledged, how long it took to be seated, and how long it took to receive your drinks, appetizers, and main course. The owners want to know if the food was hot and arranged in an appetizing manner. Generally, they are not concerned with the quality of the food as a food critic would be, but they do want to know that everything tasted fresh (the bread wasn't stale, the hamburger wasn't frozen, and so on). You are also rating the service you received, if the employee "suggestive sells" (for example: "Would you like fries with that?") and was courteous and accommodating, as well as your opinions of the atmosphere. Not if it actually suits your particular taste, but they would like to know if the music was too loud, if there was excessive dirt on the floor, and if the washrooms were clean.

With high-end restaurant shops, it helps if you have a stopwatch to assist with timings. Don't drink too much alcohol. You don't want to forget any necessary details! When you go out on these assignments, it is generally acceptable to take someone with you. Remember, you want to appear like a normal customer. Ask your scheduler if you can take a friend with you and whether you can disclose to your dining companion that this is a mystery shop. If the scheduler is okay with your friend knowing, you may be able to receive help with keeping track of timing the food delivery and other items on the assignment.

Entertainment

Amusement parks, movie theaters, golf ranges, bowling alleys, casinos, campgrounds.

Rate: Generally just reimbursement of activities for two people.

You might think these shops are all fun and games, but not to the people who want information! They're looking for reports on the courtesy of the staff, cleanliness of the area, safety issues, sound and picture quality in movie theaters, and ease of enjoyment by the customers. They want to know if you could relax and have fun, or if there were issues that made you uneasy. Was the parking lot well lit? Were the ashtrays routinely cleaned? Admittedly, these are the most fun shops to perform, as they provide opportunities to do things we like to do on our free time anyway, but keep in mind that payment for these shops is generally on a reimbursement basis. Be sure to save those receipts!

Real Estate

Apartments, new homes, retirement communities, condos.

Rate: approximately $20-$50 per shop, depending on the company and form.

These shop involve a phone call to an apartment community, a visit, and an evaluation of the community and leasing agent. In the U.S. we have fair housing laws, and apartments are shopped to make sure that they are not discriminating on age, sex, race, religion, or social status. They are also shopped by competitors to see what kinds of specials are offered, and for contests and award ceremonies given within a property management group.

For an apartment shop, you just need to pretend that you're looking for an apartment to rent or house to buy. The tricky part about apartment shops is when you have a "target." It can be difficult to get them on the phone to set an appointment. You can get around this is by requesting the target's schedule, using *67 to block your number from showing up each time you call, or getting someone to call from a different phone and tying up a line, while you try to get your agent. If you have a target, don't wait until the day your assignment is due to complete it, as you might have a hard time reaching him or her.

Unlike other types of mystery shopping assignments, you are required to be yourself during an apartment shop. There are many reasons for this. First, many agents are graded on follow-up (whether or not the agent calls you or send you a post card thanking you for stopping by). This means that you need to divulge your address and phone number. It is best to give out a PO box, or cell phone number, as you don't want your child answering the phone wondering why you're moving!

Second, when you go on apartment shops you may be required to show a photo ID. This is for the safety of the agent and the prospect. Heaven forbid something should happen during the course of an assignment, but in case something comes up, the property needs to know who is on the grounds. This doesn't mean that you can't come up with a fictitious scenario as your purpose for being on the property. When I toured many of the luxury apartment communities, I told them that I worked for Microsoft, Boeing, Ford, General Motors, and many other well-paying companies. Because let's face it, as a puppeteer, I was lucky to make $2000 a month, let alone spend that amount just on rent!

It is important to state that you are single or that your significant other is abroad (or doesn't exist), because they will not try to close the sale if they think someone else must weigh in with an opinion. You are checking to see if the leasing agent completely "qualifies" you for the community: if her or she determines the size, floor, and price range of the apartment you want, as well as if you have pets, how you heard about them, and why you're moving. The owners of the community want to know if the agent tells you about all of the features of community and apartment: the large dining area, walk-in closet, Internet access, 24-hour workout facility, seasonal pool, billiard table, free parking, free storage and so on. They want to be sure that you are told of any specials or incentives like receiving one-month free rent, free parking, or if there are contests to win a new DVD player or Ipod and so forth.

Most importantly, the agent cannot guarantee the safety of the community, nor can they tell you the age range, social or economic status, or race of current residents or neighbors. If you are asked to evaluate the fair housing laws of a community, you can ask your scheduler how to approach this topic. I have found that asking about children is acceptable in many situations since children are a protected class under the fair housing guidelines. Leasing agents should answer any question regarding the type of residents within a community by saying, "We have all kinds of people here." Their statement helps you evaluate their fair housing practices. Keep in mind that with retirement communities, you do not necessarily need to be of retirement age. You can pretend that you are looking for your mother, grandfather, great-aunt, or any other relative.

Remember, you will not actually be renting an apartment. You will follow the scenario up until the point of sale. You do not need to leave a deposit or agree to a credit or background check. It is very common for people to look at more than one apartment before they rent, and you can say you're still looking in order to leave the community without making a commitment.

Financial

Cash-checking businesses, banks, credit unions, mortgage companies, loans, FDIC insured establishments.

Rate: approximately $5-$100ish, depending on the company and form.

Financial institutions do a large volume of telephone shops, where a shopper is required only to call a branch and get information about a checking account, Money Market, or the current interest rates. In addition, there are shops to go into a branch and discuss loans or mortgages or set up accounts with a bank. There are also teller transactions, where you are required to get change or have some sort of interaction with a bank teller.

The high-end financial shops are for FDIC insurance and these require being wired with a microphone. These are extremely exclusive shops for very professional shoppers or private investigators. The rate of pay is high because the shopper is required to write down, word for word how the representative presents the programs of the institution. The financial institution is looking for information on how long it took you to meet with a representative and if he or she determined your needs and interests. They want to know if the representative clearly explained the programs that were based on your needs asked for your business, and offered additional services.

Service and Sales

Automotive, self-storage, cell phone providers, carpet cleaners, window installers.

Rate: Varies from free services like oil changes and carpet cleaning to a flat $10-$25 per form.

In these shops, you are evaluating the service provided and the representative who provides it. You state if it was done in a timely manner, that all aspects of the service or products were explained to you, and that you were satisfied with the end result. If it is an in-home evaluation, you need to comment on whether the associate was on time or gave reasonable notice for tardiness. Was he courteous in your home? Did he clarify your needs and explain how the products would suit you? If it is a store evaluation, you need to make comments about the store, noting whether items were arranged in a tasteful manner, and if there was sufficient information about the services provided. As with apartment shops, you only need to follow the assignment "up to the point of sale." You do not need to fill out a credit check form or leave a deposit.

Travel and Hospitality

Resorts, airlines, hotels, motels, cruise lines.

Rate: reimbursement for tickets or overnight accommodations and/or $10-$50 flat fee.

These are the desired shops. To be considered for these assignments first you have to find them, (remember, we're not allowed to divulge 'who shops who'!) and build a reputation with the company as a responsible shopper. It is very difficult to get high-end shops such as these when you are just starting out. You need to be confident in your shopping ability so that you don't compromise the report and lose a significant reimbursement.

In these assignments companies are looking to get feedback on the services provided. Are the rooms clean? Is the pool properly maintained? Are there enough candies in the vending machine? Were your hosts courteous? Was your wake-up call on time? Was your luggage stored properly? They may also ask you to play "hide and seek" with items in the room to make sure that the staff replenishes them the next day.

Chapter 8

Ready, Set, Go!

If You Have Access to the Internet

The easiest way to get your name out in the mystery shopping World is to go on the Internet and apply! First contact the scheduling companies and get on their lists. (Check out the Resource section for scheduling companies). Visit MSPA (**www.mysteryshop.org**), Volition **(www.volition.com)** and Jobslinger **(www.jobslinger.com)** to find assignments in your area. Apply to the companies that have open job postings first. Until you start getting into the groove of shopping, don't apply to every company that you see listed, as you might get overwhelmed. Start with 5-8, along with the scheduling companies, and go from there.

If You Do Not Have Internet Access

Admittedly, you are at a disadvantage compared with those who are online. Some mystery shopping companies are not yet on the Web, but these are smaller companies, probably just within your local area. Go to the "Market Research" section of your phone book, and call market research companies to see if they have a mystery shopping program that doesn't require Internet or e-mail. You can use your local library for Internet access and can sign up for classes to get acquainted with the technology. You might want to call the companies in the Resource section of this book to see if they do mystery shopping without the Internet. Other types of market research, such as merchandising, focus groups, or surveying, might be a good way to get yourself established with a company until you are able to get online. Once you join the Internet world, remember that your computer and Internet access are tax deductible!

In Either Case

After you have applied to be a mystery shopper, be patient. Unless the company has a job posting, it may not have work in your area at the moment you applied. Take the time to do a few sample shops to get comfortable with your duties. Go into a café, retail store, or service facility, and rate their service. Write a complete narrative from start to finish. Many companies ask for sample shops in their applications, so you will be making the process easier by completing it ahead of time. It doesn't matter if you have experience shopping. People from all walks of life are needed to do this type of work. After all, everybody shops! You will be picked for assignments if you can demonstrate that you can complete assignments on time, be completely objective, and write descriptive narrative.

Sample Application Questions

- Write a brief description of yourself.
- What cities, ZIP codes and/or area codes are you willing to shop on a regular basis?
- What are your hobbies and interests?
- What would make you a good shopper?

- What is your best shopping experience?
- What is your worst shopping experience?
- Write a narrative of your most recent shopping experience.

(Use the blank forms in the back of the book to guide you)

You might also be asked to include a resume. Don't worry if you don't have any shopping experience. Your resume should outline what you do in your "real life" since the company may be looking for people with certain backgrounds to complete various assignments.

Most mystery shopping companies will have application forms online, but should you need to send them a brief e-mail, feel free to modify the following examples:

> Greetings and Salutations,
>
> I am writing to see if you perform mystery shops in the Tallahassee, Florida area. Recently, I have done a lot of research into the mystery shopping field, and feel that I possess the qualities that are needed for the profession, including:
>
> - confidence and restraint to remain anonymous
> - keen attention to detail
> - descriptive writing style
> - flexible schedule
> - ability to meet timely and unexpected deadlines
> - responsibility to follow-through with assignments.
>
> I am interested in any type of assignment that you may offer, and would appreciate being put into your database as a shopper!
>
> Thank you so much for your consideration,
>
> -Amanda B. Reconwith

After you get some experience, and you want to contact more companies about shopping, you can modify the following letter to suit your situation:

> Greetings and Salutations,
>
> I am writing to see if you perform mystery shops in the Vancouver, BC area.
>
> I have about two years of mystery shopping experience with apartments, banks, real estate, specialty stores, movie theaters, self-storage and more! I get a lot of repeat assignments from companies as a result of my meticulous, thorough reports and quick turn over.
>
> Please let me know if you do these kinds of shops as I would like to be added to your database as a shopper.
>
> Thank you so much for your time!
>
> -Al B. Tross
> birds@youre-mail.com
> 555-555-5555

Chapter 9

Doing an Assignment

Before the Shop

You've just been given your first (or 100th) assignment! Before heading out, make sure that you go over a simple checklist. You'll want to cover all your bases in case you get lost, the target person isn't available, the store is closed, or your cell-phone dies.

Name, address and phone of the location to be shopped

You need to know where you're going and how to get there. You'd be surprised how many shoppers end up going to the wrong location of a chain store.

Scheduler information

Make sure you take any emergency phone numbers that are given to you, in case something happens and you need to reach your scheduler.

Form

Make sure you take a copy of the form with you, so you know what you're looking for. *Leave it in your car* under the seat or under a coat. You never know who will be walking by!

Telephone

Take your phone and recharger, and remember to bring change, in case your cell phone dies and you need to use a payphone.

Pens/paper/clipboard

Remember to take something to take notes on and with. A tape recorder is always good; just remember to leave it in the car unless you have specific clearance to tape recorder the employees on the assignment.

Mileage

Make sure you write down your mileage for tax deduction purposes. When you forget to write down your mileage (because it will happen) you can go to Yahoo, Google, or MapQuest after the shop and note the distance you drove.

Dress

Before going to the shop, make sure you are dressed appropriately. If you're going to a luxury apartment community, don't look scruffy. Sometimes companies will want you to dress down (for example in high-end department stores) to see if you're treated differently. They will give you these guidelines with your assignment.

Cover story

Make sure you know your cover story! Sometimes the company will give one to you; other times you will have to make it up. Regardless, make sure you know your purpose and goals for being on the assignment.

During the Shop

Your number one priority on a shop is to *remain objective and observant.* Do not let a prior experience or outside opinion influence your shop. You need to remain a "sideline observer", taking in everything that is going on in the business or community, while still coming across as a "regular" shopper. Observe how the employees interact with other customers or associates. Notice how the store is kept. All these issues will important for your evaluation.

Get the associate's name!

Take any business cards and brochures that are offered. If an associate isn't wearing a name tag, ask them what their name is. Some companies have a rule, "No name, No Pay" so be *sure* to get the first name of any associate that you talk to.

Do not lead

Be friendly and approachable but do not "lead" employees in terms of their answers. You wouldn't say, "Hi, I'm looking for a gift for my nephew, he really likes dinosaurs and the color blue, can you help me out?" You're going to have your cover story in your head…it's up to the employee to draw it out of you.

Take notes

While you're on your assignment, take a lot of mental notes, but not a lot of physical notes. If you find that you're forgetting some points, go to an area that you're not shopping such as: a different department, a restroom, or even your car to take some written notes. Do NOT take notes in front of ANY associate.

Acceptable terms

We'll discuss writing reports in the next section, but note that you will need to describe associates and some customers while on assignment. Remember your manners and refrain from using insulting descriptions such as old, fat, bald and ugly.

Keep appointments

Particularly with restaurants and real estate assignments, make sure that you keep your appointment or reservation. The company wants to know if employees were available to you at your scheduled time. The lunch hour for apartment shops is the most dubious. If you arrive 10 to 15 minutes late, your target agent may have gotten hungry and decided to go on break. Be sure to arrive 5-8 minutes within your appointed scheduled time.

Get receipts

Get in the habit of getting receipts for everything. You might need them for reimbursement, as proof that you were in the establishment, or as a tax deduction. Usually, if it's not reimbursable by the company, it's tax deductible as a business expense. Keep all your receipts and talk to a tax professional to clarify any confusion.

Have fun!

When you start mystery shopping, it can feel overwhelming trying to remember everything. Relax! This is a fun way to make some extra money, and within a few shops, you'll get the hang of it. If you want some practice, you can use the blank forms in the back of this book to do a few shops before you start taking assignments.

After the Shop

Get it out of your head

Take notes or tape-record your experience, but do not do so within view of the location. Drive down the road, pull into a parking lot, and write down the key points of your shop. If you have a tape recorder and the blank form, you can dictate the information and type it up verbatim when you get home.

Submit your report

Be sure to submit your report and any receipts within 24 hours of completion. This will result in an extremely accurate shop and a very happy scheduler! When submitting your report online, be sure to note the confirmation number, and print out or save a copy of the completed shop, should any questions arise. Keep copies of any receipts for reimbursement.

Keep in mind that your name is never used on the shopping report. You don't have to worry about a disgruntled employee tracking you down in the real world.

Log your shop

Don't forget to log the shop information in your own files. Write down when you did it, where you went, the company that you worked for, how much you should be paid, your mileage, and of course, a confirmation number. Keep your business on track by logging these simple, but important notes on a spreadsheet, in your filing system or in a software system like **www.TRIBEStrack.com.**

Chapter 10

Writing Reports

Although writing a good report can be simple when following some common-sense guidelines, this is where most shoppers fail. Here are some important "don'ts" when writing up your report.

- Don't reuse a form or cut-and-paste your answers from a previous shop. You're paid for a new report with each assignment. Honor that.
- Don't compare your current assignment with one you did earlier. Even if it's at the same location. Each shop should be evaluated on its own merit.
- Don't compare your location with the competition.
- Don't falsify your forms. You will get caught. Seriously. **You will get caught.**

When writing the evaluation, think back to your English classes and follow the basics. Always write complete sentences, avoid run-ons, use descriptive language, and check your spelling. You are hired to do a professional job, and when your reports show excellence, you will be called for more work.

Both positive and negative comments are appreciated. Many times mystery shops are the only way employees are acknowledged for providing good customer service! Keep your negative comments constructive, so that employees can be trained to do better. Remember, you're not there to get anyone fired. Simply highlight what they are doing right and how they can improve. After the report has been submitted to the client, more often than not, an employee will sit down with his or her manager to discuss it. If anything unprofessional happened, the employee will have a chance to explain.

Points to Consider When Discussing the Establishment

How does the exterior of the store look? Is the parking-lot well-kept? How does the interior look? Are products neatly displayed? Are price tags visible? Is there any debris on the floor? Are amenities clean and ready for use? Is the apartment neat and ready for move-in? What are the features of the apartment? How do the restrooms look? Are they in need of cleaning? Is there debris on the floor? Is the intercom too loud? Is the music appropriate for the establishment? Is the temperature comfortable?

Points to Consider When Discussing Associates

What are the associates doing when you enter? Are they talking about personal matters? Are they being helpful and friendly? Do they acknowledge you promptly, or do you have to approach them for assistance? Are the employees dressed in an appropriate manner? Do they offer appropriate suggestions? Do they gear the conversation to your needs and interests? Do they offer other products or services that tie in with your initial need? Do they establish rapport by engaging you in small-talk? Are incentives, discounts, or deals offered to close the sale? How do they handle your objections? Did they do anything that could have been perceived as discriminatory? If they can't answer your questions can they direct you to someone who can? Do they give you correct change for your purchase? Do they thank you and ask you to return? Do you feel that your business is appreciated? If appropriate, do they ask for contact information to follow-up with you? Did the associate try to close the sale by asking you to commit?

When discussing the associate, do not use adjectives such as fat, bald, ugly or old. Do not mention an associate's ethnicity ("African American, Caucasian, Asian"). These terms can be viewed as discriminatory and might invalidate your shop. If you are unable to get an associate's name, using a physical description should be sufficient enough, although some companies have a "no name, no pay" rule. Make sure that you are as detailed as possible, noting the age range, hair color, hair style, facial features such as a beard, moustache, glasses, height, approximate size (slender, medium, or large framed). Note any tattoos and/or piercings, and what the associate is wearing.

Use descriptive terms to give the reader a clear picture of your experience. Most forms have yes/no answers followed by a brief synopsis of events. Remember to explain all "no" answers, and give a reason for your comments. Stating "Katie was nice to talk to," doesn't give the reader a detailed picture of what happened. A better description would be: "Katie had a warm and pleasant smile and greeted me as I walked in the door. She was dressed professionally in a sharp red suit and was wearing a name-tag. She immediately shook my hand and introduced herself. Katie made me feel completely welcome and at ease by offering me refreshments of coffee and cookies." This gives the reader a dynamic sense of the encounter.

I have had the honor and privilege of editing many a shopper report, and I cannot tell you how much I hate the word NICE.

"Kathy was nice."

"The apartment was nice."

"The grounds were nice and clean."

I HATE "NICE". And so, I present to you:

Alternatives to *Nice*

Positive Words for Actions

Delightful, friendly, helpful, sincere, knowledgeable, outgoing, enthusiastic, bubbly, bright, warm, engaging, charismatic, accommodating, attentive, descriptive, efficient, cheerful, positive, agreeable, enjoyable, natural, personable, effective, polite, professional, cheery, involved, interactive, welcoming, focused.

"Nancy was delightful to talk to. She had a cheery attitude, and established rapport by engaging me in conversation about my personal interests and needs."

Negative Words for Actions

Pushy, insincere, uninterested, short, abrupt, hasty, hurried, monotonous, redundant, apathetic, interrogating, condescending, nervous, aloof, distracted, bored, vague, dry, inconsiderate, unprepared.

"Taylor was continually distracted by other associates walking by and was not focused on our interaction. He repeatedly asked me the same questions and seemed uninterested in our conversation."

Positive Words for Physical Descriptions

Clean, neat, orderly, organized, tasteful, comfortable, welcoming, open, airy, grand, expansive, colorful, bright, cheery, traditional, modern, quaint, cozy, inviting, warm.

"The apartment community is a brick mid-rise, in a 1940's style. It had large columns and looked traditional and grand. The interior reflected the style, having leather chairs seated near a fireplace, creating a warm and welcoming atmosphere."

Negative Words for Physical Descriptions

Dirty, disorganized, cramped, confining, odiferous, worn, stark, sterile, unfeeling, haphazard, in disrepair, dangerous.

"The store's interior did not give a favorable impression. The counters were worn, and the walls had no products or artwork on display. The overall feeling was quite sterile, and much of the merchandise had been rifled through, giving it a haphazard look."

Chapter 11

Sample Reports

In the next few pages, you will find example reports for the most common types of assignments. Retail, Financial, Restaurant, and Real Estate shops will be the bulk of your work when you're mystery shopping. *These forms are not the ones you will use on your assignments,* as each company uses their own forms. Some companies customize their forms for their clients, while others have standard forms.

You cannot use one company's form for another company's assignment. The ones provided here as samples are from my own business, Shop Incognito, when I ran it as a mystery shopping company.

Some forms are submitted via e-mail while others are filled out online or called in directly after the shop.

Keep in mind that when you submit your work online, some companies have "limited fields" for narrative space. This means that you can write only a certain number of characters in a box before you reach the maximum. Use language that best describes the encounter, but in as few words as possible. Companies do not necessarily appreciate a lengthy narrative, and you'll learn each company's style as you continue to work with it.

The comment sections on all of the sample forms have been expanded for your benefit! Companies will ask for a narrative of two to four sentences, not necessarily like the lengthy ones I have provided.

My writing style is reflected throughout the text of the forms and this book. It does not need to be your style as well. The most important things to remember when writing a great report are to be truthful, descriptive, objective, and accurate. Report about your experience with detail and honesty, and you will be certain to receive repeat assignments.

These forms and scenarios are completely fictional and any likeness to actual events, companies, or employees is completely coincidental and unintended.

Sample Retail Evaluation

Store name: ***Neverending Story Bookstore*** Date: ***July 27th, Saturday 2002***
Store Address: ***13456 Nothing Lane, Sebastian New York 10036***
Time Entered: ***3:30pm*** Time Left: ***3:52pm***
Associate's name/description: ***20's female, short brown hair, and glasses***
Shopper's description: ***30's female, long blonde hair, wearing jeans and a blue t-shirt***

INITIAL IMPRESSIONS

	YES	NO
Was the exterior of the store clean?	☒	☐
Was the parking lot well lit?	☒	☐
Was the store adequately lit?	☒	☐
Was the overall condition good?	☒	☐
Was the music at an appropriate level?	☒	☐
Was the merchandise well stocked?	☒	☐
Did the merchandise have price tags?	☒	☐
Were signs legible?	☒	☐
Was the floor clean?	☐	☒

COMMENTS: ***I entered The Neverending Story Bookstore at 3:30pm on Saturday 27 July. The exterior of the store was in excellent condition, with lively displays in the windows regarding summer reading programs. Since I had gone there during the day, I cannot comment on the lighting in the parking lot, but the interior of the store was well-lit. There were many large, over-stuffed couches and chairs that looked quite comfortable. The books were near on their shelves, and had price tags displayed on the covers. There was no music playing. The floors were generally clean, although I did notice that there were a few empty coffee cups near some of the chairs.***

GREETING

	YES	NO
Was your greeting prompt?	☒	☐

Time it took to be greeted: ***1-3 minutes***

	YES	NO
Were you greeted in a friendly manner?	☒	☐

Exact Greeting: ***Can I help you find something?***

Sample Retail Evaluation continued

Were there enough salespeople for the amount of traffic in the store?

YES ☒ NO ☐

COMMENTS: ***I noticed two associates at the cashier's stand assisting customers. I began to look through the books and in less than two minutes, I was approached by Bastian, who was shelving books. She greeted me in a friendly manner and offered assistance. The store was not particularly busy and seemed sufficiently staffed.***

PRODUCT PRESENTATION

ITEM REQUESTED: ***Gift for 10 year old nephew***

Did the associate determine your needs? YES ☒ NO ☐

Did they suggest an appropriate item? YES ☒ NO ☐

Item suggested: ***The book, "One Eyed Cat"***

Did they know where the item was located? YES ☒ NO ☐

Did the associate inform you of the benefits? YES ☒ NO ☐

Did the associate answer your questions? YES ☒ NO ☐

If the associate couldn't answer your questions, did they refer you to someone who could? YES ☒ NO ☐

Name and description of associate: ***Atreyu, 40's male, brown hair, large build***

Did the associate overcome your objection? YES ☒ NO ☐

Objection used, and the associate's response: ***I was concerned that the subject matter was too adult, and Atreyu offered "A Series of Unfortunate Events", telling me that his son loved the series.***

Did the associate offer other merchandise complimentary to their initial suggestion?

YES ☐ NO ☒

Item suggested: ***Atreyu did not suggest any other merchandise.***

COMMENTS: ***I told Bastian that I needed to get a gift for my nephew, who loved to read. Bastian asked how old my nephew was, and if I knew the***

Sample Retail Evaluation continued

style of books he liked to read. I told her that he was 10, but I had no idea what he liked, I just knew that he liked to read. She took me over to the young adult section, and picked out, "One-Eyed Cat" citing that it had been one of her favorites. I told her that I was concerned that it may be too "adult" for him, and she asked Atreyu, who was working in the children's section for help. Atreyu recommended, "A Series of Unfortunate Events", telling me that his son was the same age, and loved the series. At this point, Bastian excused herself to return to shelving. Atreyu told me that they had box sets of the book that were discounted. He also informed me that the purchase was fully refundable if my nephew didn't like it. He asked me if he could be of further assistance, and told me the location of the cashiers.

COMMON COURTESIES
Was the associate:

Courteous?	YES ☒	NO ☐
Respectful?	YES ☒	NO ☐

Sample Retail Evaluation...continued

Helpful?	YES ☒	NO ☐
Efficient?	YES ☒	NO ☐
Knowledgeable?	YES ☒	NO ☐

Did you feel that the associate wanted to help you?

YES ☒ NO ☐

Based on your experience, would you return?

YES ☒ NO ☐

COMMENTS: *All associates that I dealt with were pleasant and respectful. I felt that Bastian and Atreyu were very helpful and did an excellent job of determining my needs, also making good attempts at trying to fill them. The cashier was pleasant, but not particularly friendly, I would have appreciated some sort of interaction. Overall, I view this visit as a positive experience.*

Sample Retail Evaluation continued

Please tell us about your experience from beginning to end

I entered The Neverending Story Bookstore on 27 July, Saturday at 3:30pm. The exterior of the store looked clean and orderly. The interior was very welcoming, with several comfortable chairs and couches for customers to relax in. All of the shelves were neatly stocked with sufficient merchandise. The floors were clean of debris, except two empty coffee cups by some chairs.

I was greeted within 2 minutes of entering the store by Bastian, who asked if she could assist me. I told her that I needed a gift for my nephew. Bastian was in the middle of shelving books, but put down her project and asked the age of my nephew and his interests. She immediately walked me over to the young-adult section, where she recommended, "One-Eyed Cat," stating that it had been one of her favorites as a child. I was concerned that the subject matter wasn't appropriate and she took me over to Atreyu, who was working in the Children's Section. Atreyu offered, "A Series of Unfortunate Events" stating that his 10 year-old son loved it. Bastian then excused herself and went back to her shelving. Atreyu also pointed out that they had discounted box sets of the series. He asked me if he could help me further and then showed me where the cashiers were.

I waited in line for about 3 minutes before a cashier was open. The cashier greeted me with a smile, but did not engage me in small talk conversation to fill the gap of silence during the time my order was being rung up. I received a receipt and "thank you", and was able to leave the store within minutes. I was pleased with the service that I received from Atreyu and Bastian, and only wish that the cashier could have been a little more engaging. Overall, I enjoyed my shopping experience.

Sample Financial Evaluation

Branch: ***Emerald City Bank*** Date: ***15 April, Tuesday 2006***
Branch Address: ***125 Yellow Brick Lane, Kansas City, MO***
Time entered: ***1pm***
Employee's Name or Description: ***Dorothy and then Frank Baum***
Shopper's Description: ***60 yr female, medium build, short grey hair***

AT FIRST GLANCE

Was the exterior of the branch clean? YES ☒ NO ☐
Was the parking lot well maintained? YES ☒ NO ☐
Were there adequate envelopes at the ATM? YES ☒ NO ☐
Was the interior clean? YES ☒ NO ☐
How many customers were waiting in the teller line? ***three***
How many windows were open? ***two***
Were sufficient transaction slips available? YES ☒ NO ☐
How many people were at the new accounts counter? ***five***
Were there posters or displays of promotions or products?
YES ☒ NO ☐

COMMENTS: ***I first arrived at the branch and saw that the ATM was inside the vestibule of the bank. There was no debris outside, and everything looked well-maintained. The ATM was sufficiently stocked with envelopes and looked to be in working order. I entered the branch and saw that there were sufficient transaction slips available for customers. There were two tellers open and there were only 3 people waiting in line. I headed over to the customer service counter, where I saw 5 people waiting to be assisted.***

GREETING

Was your greeting/acknowledgment prompt? YES ☐ NO ☒
Time it took to be greeted: ***11-15 minutes***
Were you greeted in a friendly manner? YES ☐ NO ☒

Exact Greeting: ***"Annie Em? Is Annie Em here? Hi, Annie, Frank will be with you in a minute."***

Sample Financial Evaluation continued

COMMENTS: *There was no one at the counter, and I waited for awhile, before another customer told me to sign in. I signed in, and promptly sat down. Three of the five people waiting got up and left, and within fourteen minutes my named was called by Dorothy. Dorothy did not exactly greet me, just called my name and told me that Frank would be with me in a moment. She was not particularly friendly or welcoming.*

QUALIFYING

SERVICE REQUESTED: *New Savings Account*

Did the associate determine:

Your name?	YES ☒	NO ☐
Your contact information?	YES ☒	NO ☐
Your profession?	YES ☒	NO ☐
Where you currently bank?	YES ☒	NO ☐
The amount of funds you usually kept in your accounts?	YES ☒	NO ☐
Your purposes for the accounts?	YES ☒	NO ☐

COMMENTS: *Frank came out of his cubicle to greet me warmly with a handshake and a smile. He invited me in to have a seat and asked how he could help me. I told him that I was interested in a savings account. Frank pulled out a piece of paper to take my name, address and phone number. He also asked where I was currently banking, and what I did for a living. He did not ask why I had chosen to come into their branch that day. Frank was very pleasant and personable, and engaged me in small talk about my profession which made me feel very at ease. He asked permission to ask personal questions about my finances, and I appreciated his discretion.*

PRESENTATION

Did the associate offer a service that was suited to your needs?

YES ☒ NO ☐

Was the associate discreet when asking about sensitive financial matters?

YES ☒ NO ☐

Sample Financial Evaluation continued

Did the associate offer other products? YES ☒ NO ☐

If so, what else was offered? ***Checking accounts/ ATM/Debit cards and retirement planning.***

Did the associate seem interested in helping you? YES ☒ NO ☐

Did the associate mention interest rate and specific account information? YES ☒ NO ☐

COMMENTS: ***After determining my needs, Frank told me that they had 3 types of savings accounts available, and pulled out a brochure. The first one was a "Money Market" account where I would need to maintain a $5000 balance or pay a $15 per month fee. The second was a "Super-Savings" account that earned interest, and I would have to maintain a $1000 balance or pay a $10 fee. The third was a "Basic-Savings" account that required a $300 monthly balance, with a $3 fee should I drop below $300. Frank recommended the "Super-Savings" account based on my particular needs and asked if I wanted to set it up today. I declined, and Frank offered me a brochure explaining the savings accounts and gave me other brochures, briefly explaining that they also offered checking accounts, ATM/Debit cards, and retirement planning.***

CLOSE

Did the associate offer to set up an account today? YES ☒ NO ☐

Did the associate overcome your objection? YES ☒ NO ☐

What was your objection? ***I objected to the ATM fees, and Frank told me that none of their ATMs charged feeds to account holders.***

Did the associate offer a business card or brochure? YES ☒ NO ☐

What reason did you give for not opening an account today? ***I didn't have to give one, as Frank didn't press to have me open an account.***

How did the associate respond? ***n/a***

COMMENTS: ***Frank asked if I wanted to set up an account today, but didn't press for a reason when I declined. I told Frank that I didn't like all of the***

Sample Financial Evaluation continued

fees associated with ATM cards and Frank promptly refuted my concern by telling me that all of their ATM's were surcharge-free, and I would not have to pay a fee to use them, should I open an account. Frank asked if I had any other questions for him, and when I declined, he gave me his card and told me to feel free to contact him should I want to set up an account. Frank thanked me for coming in, and told me that he hoped to see me again soon.

ATTITUDE

Was the associate:

Pleasant?	YES ☒ NO ☐	Courteous?	YES ☒ NO ☐
Respectful?	YES ☒ NO ☐	Attentive?	YES ☒ NO ☐

If interested, would you have opened an account? YES ☒ NO ☐

Please answer why or why not: ***Although my first impression was not favorable, Frank was quite personable and friendly. He was very focused on our interaction and seemed genuinely interested in assisting me.***

If the associate could not help you, were you referred? YES ☐ NO ☒

COMMENTS: ***Frank was very sincere, personable and enthusiastic. He properly determined my needs without being pushy, and recommended appropriate services to suit them. I enjoyed dealing with him, and had I been looking in the area, I would have opened an account with Frank.***

PLEASE COMMENT ON YOUR EXPERIENCE

I first arrived at the branch and saw that the ATM was inside the vestibule of the bank. The ATM was sufficiently stocked with envelopes and looked to be in working order. I entered the branch and saw that there were two tellers open and there were only 3 people waiting in line. I headed over to the customer service counter, where I saw 5 people waiting to be assisted. There was no one at the counter, and I waited for awhile, before another customer told me to sign in. I signed in, and promptly sat down. Three of the five people waiting got up and left, and within fourteen minutes Dorothy

Sample Financial Evaluation continued

called my name. Dorothy did not exactly greet me, just called my name and told me that Frank would be with me in a moment. She was not particularly friendly or welcoming.

Frank came out of his cubicle to greet me warmly with a handshake and a smile. He invited me in to have a seat and asked how he could help me. I told him that I was interested in a savings account. Frank pulled out a piece of paper to take my name, address and phone number. He also asked where I was currently banking, and what I did for a living. He did not ask why I had chosen to come into their branch that day. Frank was very pleasant and personable, and asked permission to ask personal questions about my finances. I appreciated his discretion. After determining my needs, Frank told me that they had 3 types of savings accounts available, and pulled out a brochure. The first one was a "Money Market" account where I would need to maintain a $5000 balance or pay a $15 per month fee. The second was a "Super-Savings" account that earned interest, and I would have to maintain a $1000 balance or pay a $10 fee. The third was a "Basic-Savings" account that required a $300 monthly balance, with a $3 fee should I drop below $300. Frank recommended the "Super-Savings" account based on my particular needs and asked if I wanted to set it up today. I declined, and Frank offered me a brochure explaining the savings accounts and gave me other brochures, briefly explaining that they also offered checking accounts, ATM/Debit cards, and retirement planning. I told Frank that I didn't like all of the fees associated with ATM cards and Frank promptly refuted my concern by telling me that all of their ATM's were surcharge-free, and I would not have to pay a fee to use them, should I open an account. Frank asked if I had any other questions for him, and when I declined, he gave me his card and told me to feel free to contact him should I want to set up an account. Frank thanked me for coming in, shook my hand, and told me that he hoped to see me again soon.

Frank was very sincere, personable and enthusiastic. He properly determined my needs without being pushy, and recommended appropriate services to suit them. I enjoyed dealing with him, and had I been looking in the area, I would have opened an account with Frank.

Sample Restaurant Evaluation

Date: ***30 July 2003***	Day and Time: ***Sunday 6pm***
Location: ***Willies Chocolate Palace***	Server: ***Veruca***
Address: ***58623 Oompa Loompa Drive, Beauregard, LA 89456***	
Number in party: ***2***	Total Score: ***150***
Service Score: ***102***	Location Score: ***48***

INITIAL IMPRESSIONS (please rate 1-5)
5 Did the restaurant make a welcoming impression from the street?
5 Was the exterior of the restaurant clean?
5 Was the parking lot well lit?
5 Did the landscaping look well-maintained?

COMMENTS: *The exterior of the restaurant was clean and inviting. It gives the impression of a circus or carnival. There were bright lights and bright colors that led to the entrance. The parking lot was well lit, and just walking from the car I immediately knew I would be in for an adventure!*

ATMOSPHERE (please rate 1-5)
5 Was the music at an appropriate level?
5 Were the staff dressed in uniform?
5 Was lighting at an appropriate level?
5 Was the interior of the restaurant inviting?
5 Were the aisles easy to maneuver around?
5 Were restroom signs clearly noted?

COMMENTS: *The atmosphere of the restaurant was very welcoming. The music was very cheery, ranging from big-band, to calliope and was at an appropriate level. All visible staff were in uniforms that were brightly colored and added to the festive theme.*

HOST STAND (Please rate 1-5)
Host Name: *Augustus* Time Entered: *6pm*
How many guests were in line to be seated? *3*

Sample Restaurant Evaluation continued

Were you put on a waiting list? *no*

5 Did the host greet you in a friendly manner?

5 Was the host appropriately dressed?

5 Did the host determine your seating preference?

5 If an estimate time was given, was it met?

COMMENTS: *We entered the restaurant at 6 pm and saw three groups of guests waiting to be seated. We were greeted in a friendly manner by Augustus, who was wearing a uniform and a name tag. Augustus asked how many in our party, and our seating preference and then told us that it would be about another 20 minutes before a table was ready. We were seated within 15 minutes.*

AT THE TABLE (please rate 1-5)

Server: *Veruca* Time Sat: *6:15pm* Time Greeted: *6:20pm*

5 Was the table set with the appropriate amount of flatware?

5 Were the salt and pepper shakers filled?

5 Did the server greet you in a friendly manner?

5 Did the server offer you his/her name?

5 Did the server offer you something from the bar?

5 Did the server check for photo ID, (if under 35)

Bar items ordered: *Amaretto Sour, Fizzylifting Soda*

COMMENTS: *Veruca approached our table promptly, introducing herself and offering beverages to "start off with". She was very outgoing and personable and dressed appropriately in uniform with a name tag. Veruca took our bar order, and returned within 5 minutes to deliver our drinks and take our order. We ordered an Amaretto Sour and a Fizzylifting Soda. Both drinks were prepared well and had a fine taste.*

ORDERING (please rate 1-5)

0 Did the server offer appetizers?

2 Were the daily specials noted?

Sample Restaurant Evaluation continued

__2__ Was the server able to answer questions you had about the entrees?
Entrees ordered: ***The Snozzberry Special, The Gobbstopper Gobbler***

COMMENTS: ***Veruca did not offer appetizers, nor tell us about the daily specials. She mentioned that if we were interested there was a special board by the fountain. We ordered the Snozzberry Special and the Gobbstopper Gobbler.***

DELIVERY OF FOOD (please rate 1-5)
TIME ORDER RECEIVED: ***6.40pm***

__*5*__ Did you receive what you had ordered?
__*5*__ Was the presentation of the food favorable?
__*5*__ Was the food tasteful?
__*5*__ Did the server offer complimentary items?
__*5*__ Did the server offer to refill beverages?

COMMENTS: ***Veruca promptly delivered our order, remembering what each person had asked for. The food looked delicious, and was arranged in an appetizing manner. The food was tasty and not too hot or cold. Veruca offered to refill our beverages and asked if we needed anything else.***

FOLLOW UP (please rate 1-5)
TIME SERVER CHECKED BACK: ***6.48pm***
__*1*__ Did the server offer dessert?
Time it took to receive dessert: ***did not order dessert***
__*1*__ Did the server offer after dinner drinks?
Time it took to receive after dinner drinks: ***did not order drinks***
__*5*__ Did the server or busser clear empty plates?

COMMENTS: ***Veruca checked back with us about 8 minutes after she delivered our order and asked how everything was. She asked if we needed anything else, and when we declined, she told us she would be back with our***

Sample Restaurant Evaluation continued

Bill. She then cleared some of our empty plates out of the way. She did not specifically ask if we wanted dessert or drinks.

RECEIVING THE BILL (please rate 1-5)
TIME SERVER DROPPED OFF BILL: ***6.55pm***
5 Did the bill have the correct amount charged?
5 Did the server leave any promotional items (i.e., mints) with the bill?

COMMENTS: ***Veruca dropped off our bill with mints, and asked us once again if we needed anything else. She then cleared some more of our empty plates, and told us that she would be happy to take the bill up to the front for us when we were ready.***

TIME RECEIPT WAS RECEIVED: ***7.02pm***

PLEASE RATE OUR MANNER (please rate 1-5)

	Your Host	Your Server	Other Staff
Friendliness	*5*	*5*	*n/a*
Helpfulness	*5*	*5*	*n/a*
Sincerity	*5*	*5*	*n/a*
Courtesy	*5*	*5*	*n/a*
Knowledge	*5*	*3*	*n/a*

Please note the other staff you came in contact with: *n/a*.

5 Based on your experience, would you return?

Why or why not? ***The staff was very personable and accommodating, the food was excellent and delivered in a timely fashion. Veruca received a 3 rating on knowledge only because she did not tell us about the specials, but left it up to us to seek out the special board by the fountain.***

Sample Restaurant Evaluation continued

PLEASE RATE OUR DINING ROOM (please rate 1-5)

	Dining Room	Bar/Lounge	Restroom
Floors	*5*	*5*	*5*
Seats/Stalls	*5*	*5*	*5*
Tables/Counters	*5*	*5*	*3*
Courtesy	*5*	*5*	*5*
Supplies	*5*	*5*	*5*

PLEASE COMMENT ON OUR FACILITIES

The dining room had a great atmosphere of fun and amusement. The physical condition was well-kept, as there was no debris on the floor. The entryway was grand and comfortable, and there was enough seating for people waiting for tables. Our table was wiped down and sufficiently stocked with condiments. The chairs in both the dining area and the lounge were colorful and looked new. The women's restroom was evaluated for this assignment. Overall, it looked to be in excellent condition. There were adequate supplies in the stalls, and there was no debris on the floor. The garbage cans were tidy and were not overflowing. There were 3 sinks, all of which had a minor amount of water around the basin.

Sample Real Estate Evaluation

Property: ***Wonderland Apartments*** Leasing Agent: ***Alice***
Date: ***3 January 2003*** Day: ***Tuesday*** Shopper ID: ***14541***
COVER STORY Size apartment desired: ***one-bedroom***
Date moving: ***15 January 2003*** Employer: ***Mad Hatter Productions***
Currently live: ***Carroll, WI*** Number of residents: ***one***
Reason for Moving: ***New to the area***
Advertising Source Used: ***The "Looking Glass Times" classifieds***

TELEPHONE CONSULTATION

Property: ***Wonderland Apartments*** Leasing Agent: ***Alice***
Date of Call: ***3 January 2003*** Time of Call: ***11am***

__2__ How many attempts did it take to reach your target/leasing agent?
Describe your attempts to reach the office and your target: ***The first time I called was at 10am on 3 January. Lewis answered the phone. I told him that I had a wrong number, and called back one hour later. I then reached Alice.***

PLEASE TELL US ABOUT THE GREETING
How many rings to answer the phone? ***two***
Were you placed on hold? ***no*** For how long? ***n/a***
Did the agent have a memorable greeting?
YES ☒ NO ☐
What was the agent's greeting? ***It's a Wonderful Day at Wonderland!***
Did the agent state the name of the property? YES ☒ NO ☐
Did the agent offer his/her name? YES ☒ NO ☐
Did the agent ask for your name? YES ☒ NO ☐

COMMENTS: ***Alice answered the phone promptly and professionally within two rings. She answered enthusiastically stating, "It's a Wonderful Day at Wonderland!" I was not placed on hold during our conversation. Alice introduced the property and herself and asked for my name.***

PLEASE TELL US ABOUT THE QUALIFICATION PROCESS

Sample Real Estate Evaluation continued

Did the agent...

Ask when you needed an apartment?	YES ☒	NO ☐
Ask the size you needed?	YES ☒	NO ☐
Ask your price range?	YES ☒	NO ☐
Ask the number of residents?	YES ☒	NO ☐
Ask about pets?	YES ☒	NO ☐
Ask about your work?	YES ☒	NO ☐
Ask about the ad source?	YES ☒	NO ☐
Ask why you were moving?	YES ☒	NO ☐

If your needs couldn't be met, were you referred to another community?

YES ☐ N/A ☒ NO ☐

COMMENTS: ***Alice did an excellent job of qualifying me. She determined when I was moving, the size apartment I wanted, the number of occupants, if I had pets, my price range, where I was currently living and working, how I had heard about them, why I was moving, and my specific needs in my "new apartment home".***

PLEASE TELL US ABOUT THE AGENT'S PRESENTATION

Did the agent...

Describe the features of the apartment?	YES ☐	NO ☒
Offer the square footage?	YES ☐	NO ☒
Describe the features of the community?	YES ☐	NO ☒
Describe the area conveniences?	YES ☐	NO ☒
Offer the price?	YES ☐	NO ☒
Offer a promotion or incentive to visit?	YES ☒	NO ☐

COMMENTS: ***Alice did not tell me the price or square footage of the apartment. She did not inform me of the apartment or community features. Nor did she tell me about the area where they were located. Alice did tell me that they were currently offering one month free rent.***

PLEASE TELL US ABOUT THE CLOSE

Sample Real Estate Evaluation continued

Did the agent…

Ask you to visit the property?	YES ☒	NO ☐
Offer an appointment time?	YES ☒	NO ☐
Offer clear directions?	YES ☒	NO ☐
Ask for your contact information?	YES ☒	NO ☐
Thank you for calling?	YES ☒	NO ☐

COMMENTS: ***Alice offered an in-person tour, and we set a specific appointment time. She offered clear directions to the property and took my phone number. Before ending the conversation on a pleasant note, Alice thanked me for calling and confirmed our appointment time.***

PLEASE TELL US ABOUT THE AGENT'S MANNER

Did the agent…

Control over the conversation?	YES ☒	NO ☐
Seem natural on the phone?	YES ☒	NO ☐
Direct the call to your interests?	YES ☐	NO ☒
Create a sense of urgency to visit?	YES ☒	NO ☐
Seem genuinely interested in helping you?	YES ☒	NO ☐

COMMENTS: ***Alice had an excellent control over the conversation. She was very natural and personable, and seemed interested in talking with me. She did not give me enough information to make me interested in seeing the apartment, but did offer an incentive to visit by telling me that they were offering one month free, and new residents were entered into a drawing for a new DVD player or VCR.***

ON SITE EVALUATION

Property: ***Wonderland Apartments*** Leasing Agent: ***Alice***

Date: ***3 January 2003*** Day: ***Tuesday*** Arrival Time: ***1pm***

PLEASE TELL US ABOUT YOUR INITIAL IMPRESSIONS

Did you easily find the community?	YES ☒	NO ☐

Sample Real Estate Evaluation continued

Were signs visible to the leasing office?	YES ☒	NO ☐
Were signs/banners in good condition?	YES ☒	NO ☐
Were the buildings in good condition?	YES ☐	NO ☒
Was the parking lot clear and free of debris?	YES ☐	NO ☒
Was the landscaping in good condition?	YES ☐	NO ☒
Was your first impression of the community good?	YES ☐	NO ☒

COMMENTS: ***The property was easy to locate. There is a large sign from the main road. The rental office was located right at the entrance. The exterior of the property did not give a favorable impression. I saw debris on the ground, in the parking lots, and a lot of paint chipping off of the buildings.***

PROPERTY EVALUATION

PLEASE TELL US ABOUT THE OFFICE CONDITION

Was the office open, clean and ready for business?	YES ☒	NO ☐
Was the office desk area neat and organized?	YES ☒	NO ☐
Were the Fair Housing/Rental Requirements posted?	YES ☒	NO ☐

COMMENTS: ***The office was clean and open and in excellent condition. The desks were neat and organized. The office gave a very favorable first impression, and was tastefully decorated.***

WERE THE APARTMENT FEATURES IN GOOD CONDITION?

Walls and paint	YES ☒	NO ☐
Carpeting	YES ☒	NO ☐
Windows/blinds	YES ☒	NO ☐
Bathroom: floor, toilet, sink, mirror, cabinets	YES ☒	NO ☐
Kitchen: floor, sink, cabinets, appliances	YES ☐	NO ☒
Closets	YES ☒	NO ☐
Lights	YES ☒	NO ☐
Balcony	YES ☐	NO ☒
Stairs, interior and/or exterior	YES ☐	NO ☒

Sample Real Estate Evaluation continued

COMMENTS: ***The staircase to the apartment look liked it needed repair, and the apartment itself, although clean, was in need of a kitchen drawer, and maintenance on the balcony.***

PLEASE TELL US ABOUT THE PROPERTY CONDITION

List amenities available and whether you viewed them

Clubhouse	YES ☒	NO ☐	VIEWED ☒
Pool/Jacuzzi	YES ☒	NO ☐	VIEWED ☒
Sauna	YES ☐	NO ☒	VIEWED ☐
Exercise room	YES ☒	NO ☐	VIEWED ☒
Office Center	YES ☐	NO ☒	VIEWED ☐
Outdoor tennis/basketball courts	YES ☐	NO ☒	VIEWED ☐
Racquetball courts	YES ☐	NO ☒	VIEWED ☐
Laundry Room	YES ☐	NO ☒	VIEWED ☐

Other: ***I did not learn of any other amenities during my tour.***

Did the property give a favorable impression overall? YES ☐ NO ☒

COMMENTS: ***The amenities of the property were clean and in excellent condition. The exterior of the property did not give a favorable impression. I saw debris on the ground, and a lot of paint chipping off of the buildings.***

PLEASE TELL US ABOUT YOUR ONSITE GREETING

Did the agent…

Acknowledge you promptly?	YES ☒	NO ☐
Smile and stand to greet you?	YES ☒	NO ☐
Introduce him or herself?	YES ☒	NO ☐
Offer you a seat or refreshments?	YES ☒	NO ☐
Remember your phone call?	YES ☒	NO ☐
Shake your hand and ask your name?	YES ☒	NO ☐
Use your name throughout the tour?	YES ☒	NO ☐

Sample Real Estate Evaluation continued

COMMENTS: ***Alice was on the phone when I entered, but acknowledged me with a smile and a motion to come in. When she ended the conversation, she smiled, shook my hand, verified my name, and introduced herself. She also thanked me for waiting so patiently, and offered me some water.***

PLEASE TELL US ABOUT YOUR ONSITE QUALIFICATION

Did the Agent use a welcome card, ask you to fill one out, or ask:

a) date desired	YES ☒	NO ☐
b) size needed	YES ☒	NO ☐
c) number of occupants	YES ☒	NO ☐
d) if you had pets	YES ☒	NO ☐
e) where you were working	YES ☒	NO ☐
f) where you were living	YES ☒	NO ☐
g) why you were moving	YES ☒	NO ☐
h) your contact information	YES ☒	NO ☐
Did the agent ask for any special needs?	YES ☒	NO ☐

COMMENTS: ***Alice began filling out a welcome card with information that she had remembered from our phone conversation. She verified all of my interests, asked if I had any special needs.***

PLEASE TELL US ABOUT THE PRE-TOUR

Did the Agent…

Show you floor plans?	YES ☒	NO ☐	
Show you the apartment on the community map?	YES ☒	NO ☐	

If no vacancies were available for showing, did the agent:

a) show you floor plans?	YES ☐	NO ☐	N/A ☒
b) show you a model?	YES ☐	NO ☐	N/A ☒
c) show you an occupied apartment?	YES ☐	NO ☐	N/A ☒
d) invite you back for another tour?	YES ☐	NO ☐	N/A ☒

Did the agent ask for photo I.D. before showing apartment?

YES ☒ NO ☐

Sample Real Estate Evaluation continued

COMMENTS: ***Alice showed me floor plans of the apartment, and a brochure depicting where it was located within the community. She took my photo ID before we started on the tour.***

PLEASE TELL US ABOUT THE AGENT'S DEMONSTRATION

Did you see a model, vacant apartment, neither, or both?

M ☐ **V** ☒ **N** ☐ **B** ☐

Please list the number of the apartment(s) shown: ***L204***

Did the agent…

Have a good conversation control?	YES ☒	NO ☐
Mention onsite staff or maintenance?	YES ☒	NO ☐
Discuss the property benefits?	YES ☒	NO ☐
Show all recreation areas?	YES ☒	NO ☐
Discuss the area benefits?	YES ☒	NO ☐
Demonstrate the features of the unit?	YES ☒	NO ☐
Increase the value? (paid utilities, etc)	YES ☒	NO ☐
Use your name throughout the tour?	YES ☒	NO ☐
Seem rushed or hurried?	YES ☐	NO ☒

COMMENTS: ***Alice had an excellent presentation. She maintained control throughout the tour, talking about the staff, the amenities and location conveniences. She also created rapport by asking me about my work and interests. Alice thoroughly demonstrated the amenities of the property, and the apartment, and took the time to answer any questions I had.***

PLEASE TELL US ABOUT YOUR OBJECTIONS AND THE CLOSE

Did the agent…

Ask closing questions throughout tour?	YES ☒	NO ☐
Create a sense of urgency	YES ☒	NO ☐
Attempt to overcome your objections?	YES ☒	NO ☐

Sample Real Estate Evaluation continued

What was your objection, and how did the agent overcome it?
I objected to the condition of the apartment, and Alice said that it would be ready by the time I moved in.

Seem comfortable with the price?	YES ☒	NO ☐
Explain any move-in costs and fees?	YES ☒	NO ☐
Did the agent attempt a close?	YES ☒	NO ☐
Did the agent attempt a second close?	YES ☒	NO ☐
How did the agent ask you to commit?		
a) by filling out an application	YES ☒	NO ☐
b) by leaving a deposit	YES ☒	NO ☐
c) by leaving a hold	YES ☐	NO ☒
d) by renting the apartment	YES ☒	NO ☐
Did the agent offer incentives to rent?	YES ☒	NO ☐

How did the agent react to you not renting the apartment? ***Alice asked me why, and I told her that I was still looking around. She told me that I wouldn't find a deal like this anywhere else and continued to try and close me. After awhile, I became uncomfortable with her pushiness.***

COMMENTS: ***Alice asked closing questions throughout the tour and created a sense of urgency by offering one month free, and mentioning that they only had one apartment available. She asked if I wanted to rent the apartment, if I wanted to leave a deposit, or if I wanted to fill out an application. Alice tried to close me several times, and by the end of the tour, I felt that she was being a little pushy.***

PLEASE TELL US ABOUT THE AGENT'S ATTITUDE AND APPEARANCE

Was the agent…

Enthusiastic, genuine, and attentive?	YES ☒	NO ☐
Natural and not rehearsed?	YES ☒	NO ☐
Able to establish a rapport with you?	YES ☒	NO ☐
Dressed in an appropriate manner?	YES ☒	NO ☐

Sample Real Estate Evaluation continued

Professional at all times? YES ☒ NO ☐
Discriminatory in any way? YES ☐ NO ☒

Was an apartment available in the size you wanted? YES ☒ NO ☐
Were you shown that apartment? YES ☒ NO ☐
Were you encouraged to live in a particular part of the community?
YES ☐ NO ☒

COMMENTS: *Alice was dressed appropriately and professionally and had a great attitude. She kept me interested in the tour by informing me about what they had to offer. Alice continually asked me if I was interested in renting, where else I was looking, when I would make a decision, and this added pressure made me feel a bit on edge. I thought that she had a professional attitude, but would have appreciated a more relaxed approach.*

PLEASE TELL US ABOUT YOUR OVERALL EXPERIENCE *Alice answered the phone with enthusiasm and flair. She properly determined all of my needs, right down to my preference of carpeting color, and did so in a conversational manner. Alice created a sense of urgency by telling me that they were offering one month free and also giving away a DVD player or VCR. Alice then invited me out to view the community, and asked for my phone number. We set an appointment time, and she gave me clear and concise directions. As she was ending the conversation, Alice thanked me for calling, and told me to have a pleasant day. Alice did not tell me about the apartment or community, their features or amenities, and I would have appreciated this information prior to the tour. Otherwise, Alice had a very professional and personable telephone demeanor.*

The community is an older property, and looks to be in need of some work. The buildings are brown, with dark brown trim and bright white garages. I saw a lot of paint chipping off of the buildings, the curbs and the balconies. Overall, the property did not give a very favorable impression. Alice was on the phone when I entered, and was able to assist me within a reasonable

Sample Real Estate Evaluation continued

time frame. She remembered our conversation, and sat down with me to go over my needs and interests by filling out a welcome card. Her manner was very pleasant and perky, and I enjoyed talking with her.

Alice first showed me a vacant apartment. On the way to the apartment, she engaged me in conversation, and I was able to learn more of how the community could suit me through its amenities. The staircase to the apartment was also in need of repair. It looked like some of the wood was rotting. The apartment itself was spacious and clean. It was in need of a drawer in the kitchen and the balcony also needed some maintenance work. I objected to these conditions, and Alice told me that they could have everything fixed by the time I was ready to move in, but this was the only apartment that they had available. Alice then showed me the amenities, which were clean and appealing. I saw the pool, spa, workout room, sauna, and tanning bed. All were in great condition and ready for use.

Alice asked closing questions throughout the tour. She asked me where else I had been looking and when I was going to make my decision. She asked me twice to put a hold on the apartment, and once to fill out an application. Alice also gave me a business card and brochure to take with me. Alice quite persistent, and when I declined again, she asked me why I was so hesitant. I told her that I had just begun my search, and that there were other apartments that I was going to go look at. Alice asked me where else I was looking, and I gave the names of two communities in the area. Alice went over, in detail, how her community would suit me better, and then asked again if I wanted to fill out an application or at least take one with me. When I declined, she gave me a "coupon," stating that if I returned within 72 hours, I would get $50 off the move in costs. By the end of the tour, I felt that Alice was being pushy, and I was not comfortable with how she kept asking me for a commitment. During the course of the tour she was very personable and approachable, and I thoroughly enjoyed our conversation. At the end of the tour she became fairly intense. Had she not been so persistent with the closing, I would have rented an apartment from Alice.

Chapter 12

Getting More Assignments

Say you've been shopping for a while but aren't getting the volume of assignments that you want. It could be that there just aren't as many assignments in your area, especially if you don't live near a major city, but before you give up on mystery shopping altogether, try these suggestions first:

Check Your E-mail

Most schedulers and companies contact their shoppers via e-mail. Check your e-mail several times a week, if not several times daily. If you use your cell phone to access the web, set it up so that you can receive notices of when you get emails as well.

Check Job Boards

The companies that have job boards on their sites rarely send out e-mail notices about upcoming assignments. They don't have to since most of their shoppers will self-assign shops. Put it in your weekly (or daily) routine to check the job boards to see what assignments are available.

Check Social Media Sites

Many companies are now moving towards using Twitter and Facebook to post assignments. Generally these are last minute assignments that another shopper dropped. Sign up for Twitter and Facebook to get quick notices of last minute (and possibly bonus) assignments!

If You Like It – GRAB IT!

If you receive a notice about an assignment or see something you'd like to do on a job board, don't hesitate: GRAB IT! For specialty and fun assignments, this is especially necessary. Other shoppers want the fun shops as well, so if you want to do it, and you CAN do it, don't wait. Go for it!

Apply to More Companies

There are hundreds of companies that you can work with. Once you've exhausted the listings in the back of this book, you can find more in your phone book under "Market Research." You can also find more listings and job assignments through the MSPA, Volition, and Job Slinger (**www.mysteryshop.org**, **www.volition.com**, **www.jobslinger.com**).

Try Different Things

Don't be afraid to try opportunities other than mystery shopping. Go out and find merchandising, surveying, mock trials, auditing, focus groups, and other types of market research. If you really want to expand your knowledge base, read my book, *I Got Scammed So You Don't Have To*! which presents over 300 ideas and resources for you to find legitimate work-at-home and random jobs while avoiding the tricks of scammers.

Visit **www.QueenoftheRandomJob.com** for more information.

Check Back with Companies You Haven't Heard From

If you haven't heard from a company for a few weeks after you've applied, contact it again to check your status. Give the company some time, though. It has lots of mystery shoppers and won't necessarily appreciate those who nag for work.

Sign Up with Assignment Services

There are several companies that specialize in helping shoppers get more assignments. There is a fee to sign up, but you will receive e-mail from schedulers and mystery shopping companies about available assignments. You definitely do NOT need to sign on with these companies, but they are available to you, if you wish to use their services.

Expand Your Travel Route

If you're going out of town or are willing to drive farther, let your companies know. Sometimes it's worth the extra tax-deduction of mileage to pick up shops that are farther away from your home. I once agreed to do 6 apartment shops 90 minutes away from my home. It was a very long day (15 hours) but the $300 I made was totally worth the time and effort.

Get MSPA Certification

The MSPA has a training course that covers the basics of mystery shopping. When you pass, you receive a certificate number that you can then put in your mystery shopping applications. By going through training, you're showing the mystery shopping companies that you are serious about the quality of work you provide. There is debate whether certification is worth it, and I discuss it at length in the "Paying to Shop?" chapter of this book.

Do Good Work

It goes without saying that in order to be considered for more work, you need to conduct yourself in a professional manner. Make sure that you submit your reports on time and that they are accurate, descriptive, and reflective of your best effort.

Chapter 13

Breaking the Myths

Mystery shopping can be a lot of fun and a great way to make a part-time income, but there are drawbacks. Make sure that you have realistic expectations when beginning your mystery shopping career, so that you don't get sucked into the notion that the work is "easy money."

Social Security Numbers

You will have to give your social security number in order to work for mystery shopping companies. Just like filling out an application at any regular job, this information is required in order to process payment.

If you make over $599 with any one company over the course of a year, it is legally required to send a 1099 form to the IRS. If you make less than that, you'll still need to declare the income, but the company doesn't have to file the paperwork.

Since a lot of applying can be done online, you will have to give out this information over the Internet. Make sure that the site is secure! In the address bar you should see an "https://" and a closed yellow lock at the bottom of the screen (depending on which browser you use). "Secure" means that when you hit "submit," your information be encrypted and encoded while it's transmitting over the Internet, and go directly into a company's database. No one can tap into it during submission, and no employee deals with it until payroll or tax processing. If you are uncomfortable with this, contact the shopping company by phone and ask how to submit your information a different way.

Sporadic Assignments

Assignments are only available when mystery shopping companies receive contracts to do them. This means that you might receive a ton of work one month, but the next month may have a hard time finding assignments. It is a fickle industry, and after a few "dry" months, you might become frustrated.

Keep in mind that you will never receive the same number of assignments each month from each company you are working for. That's just not how it works. Shoppers are needed on rotation. You can't go into the same store every month; you'll get caught!

The more companies that you apply to, the more offers for assignments you'll receive. It may take a little while to get started because you're battling the "flake factor." There are thousands of people who are trying to be mystery shoppers, and thousands of people who don't realize that this is a job, and you need to provide good work. Schedulers may be wary just because you're new, but once you show them that you're reliable, you'll be contacted time and time again.

The first month that I was mystery shopping, I did one assignment. The second, I did two, and then it grew from there. I never knew from month to month exactly how much money I'd be making from each company. Some I only heard from twice a year, others, I heard from on an almost daily basis. The good part about mystery shopping is that it is flexible, the bad part is that you may not get as much work as you want when you want it. Don't rely on mystery shopping for your mortgage payment! This is fun, flexible income, but it's not necessarily consistent.

Competition

People always wonder if the Mystery Shopper market is flooded and if they have a chance against others out there who may have more experience, flexibility, or charm. Keep in mind that people have different schedules. Some are interested in mystery shopping as a hobby, only shopping restaurants and movies. Other people want to make money at it by specializing in assignments that don't require expenses. Some people can only shop on the weekend, and other people can only shop during the week. You should never shop the same location within 3-4 months of a completed assignment for risk of giving yourself away. (I recommend at least six months between apartment shops.)

Assignments are constantly being rotated, so if you are declined for a shop one month, you could pick it up the next. There's more than enough opportunity out there for everyone! That being said, if you find an assignment that you would like, TAKE IT IMMEDIATELY! It may be gone if you don't grab it, and then you'll have to wait until it comes up again.

All that schedulers and mystery shopping companies want are shoppers who are reliable, follow directions, and write clear, descriptive reports. Believe it or not, it can be VERY difficult to simply find these people. There's so much information on the Internet regarding mystery shopping, and most people don't understand that it's a serious business. If you do good work, and are pleasant to work with, you *will* be called for more assignments. Any company will tell you that good Mystery Shoppers are *golden*.

Getting Paid What You're Worth

There is a huge debate among mystery shoppers regarding the fees that they are paid. A lot of professional Mystery Shoppers will not take the lower-end assignments that may pay about $5-$8, because it isn't worth their time. New shoppers will sometimes be more than happy to take the assignments, because they want to get established and they may not know any better.

Established shoppers are often concerned that mystery shopping companies will lower their payment rates because so many new shoppers are constantly entering the field.

My advice is simple: if you do not feel that the assignment is worth the time you will have to put into it (including how long it took you to find the assignment, travel, gas, writing the report, and any associated costs), don't take it. Total up your drive time, being at the location, driving home and writing up the report. If you're making less than $10-12 per hour, then you probably can let that assignment go.

I have taken assignments thinking that the compensation was fair, only to realize later that with the length of the form, or the drive time, or extra time spent at the location, my effort wasn't really worth it. These were learning experiences, and you will have some of your own. Only you can decide what assignments are worth it to you. I know people who won't touch fast-food places with a ten-foot pole, and I know single moms who say, "Heck, yeah! Give me three on the way home. That's dinner!" It'll take you a while to figure out your own groove and decide what is worth your time, expertise, and effort.

Mystery shoppers provide an invaluable service. Businesses can't get the in-depth information that shoppers provide through those little comment cards. And most customers won't take the time to contact a company to let them know how they felt about their experience, unless it was extremely good or bad. Mystery shoppers give companies an honest, in-depth view on how employees are really treating customers and prospects. Businesses receive accurate and timely report of how regular people view their establishment, atmosphere, and services, and there is no reason why you can't get paid what you're worth!

Chapter 14

What If You Get Caught?

Getting caught is no fun. Not only does it mean that you won't get paid, but you compromise your anonymity! Getting caught does happen to the best of us and most businesses perform evaluations let their employees know that they have shopping programs. It's not a complete surprise for employees to find out that they have been shopped.

When you get caught, the employee will probably tell all of his coworkers. Then the manager finds out. The manager or owner (whoever ordered the shop) contacts the shopping company to let it know that the shop is invalid. The shop needs to be rescheduled, but obviously it can't be done any time soon, as all the employees will be on heightened alert. When you get caught, it wastes time and money for everyone involved, so here are some tips to help you avoid this situation:

Getting Caught by an Employee

Don't panic. Breathe. Act confused, act befuddled, but most importantly, act like you've never heard the words "mystery shopping". Do NOT say "Mystery shopper? No, I'm not a mystery shopper!" Because automatically the employee will think: "Oh, yes, you are!"

You want to be viewed as a regular customer no matter what happens. Let the associate give a full explanation of what a mystery shopper does and feel free to ask questions! Say that you think that sounds fun and ask how you can get started! Do NOT confess to being a mystery shopper, or even admit that you know people who are shoppers. If you're able to pull off your supposed ignorance, you might still be able to get paid. If the shop is faltering, and you think that there is no hope of maintaining your anonymity, finish the shop as assigned and contact your scheduler immediately. The result may invalidate the shop, but it's more important to protect your reputation as a shopper than it is to miss payment on one shop. Companies appreciate honesty, and you will have earned their respect by telling them what happened.

Getting Caught by a Friend

Yes, it can happen. There you are trying to do your job, and there is Aunt Phyllis or Uncle Phil, wondering why on earth you are in their favorite restaurant eating alone! In most cases, this can be easy to pull off, as it may not seem strange if you're in a restaurant, retail store, or movie theater. If you are dealing with a salesperson, however, and an acquaintance is approaching, it is always best to keep your cover story reasonably legitimate, so that you, or anyone else, can believe it. For example, don't tell the sales associate that you're looking for a gift for your child, if you don't actually have children.

A difficult situation might come up if you are caught apartment shopping. If you run into a friend, they might ask why on earth you've dumped your spouse and decided to rent a one-bedroom apartment! If it happens, remember to breathe, stay calm and think on your feet. Remember that if you divulge your true purpose you will be breaking your confidentially agreement.

On one assignment, I ran into a friend of an old boyfriend's, who I hadn't seen in 3 years. She was working as a temp at the apartment building I was shopping. I didn't have my appointment with her, but she definitely made a scene when I arrived. This was a luxurious apartment community (think $2,000 apartments) and she knew that I was a broke puppeteer with no business being in such a community. She even had the nerve to snidely say to me: "Well! It looks like your financial situation has improved!" Which was a bit embarrassing considering that I was there trying to get an apartment. I was able to keep my cool (although I was more than annoyed with her presence) and tell her that I was indeed working for a marketing agency downtown. Which was my cover story for the shop and also partly true (I was Ronald McDonald's bodyguard at the time, not really working for the agency).

In this particular case I was thankful that I hadn't used my typical cover story when shopping luxurious apartments in Seattle. Usually I told people I worked for Microsoft, and the woman I ran into had worked there for several years, and also knew I didn't have a clue about computers. In the end, the leasing agent had no idea that I was a shopper, as I pulled everything off without a hitch. Even my nosy former friend bought my story. Chalk one up to those improvisational acting classes!

Chapter 15

When Shops Go Wrong

While you're out on the town and shopping up a storm, you are going to encounter bizarre situations that you couldn't ever have imagined. The weirdest stuff is going to happen. Guaranteed.

When shops go wrong, there are some basic scenarios where common sense is called for:

- If you can't complete a shop, you need to tell your scheduler immediately.
- If you get caught, you need to remain as anonymous as possible on the assignment and then tell your scheduler what happened.
- If an employee is rude or unsavory, you need to keep your cool; you're at work and you need to retain your professionalism.
- The most common mishap in apartment shops is when your target leasing agent passes you off to someone else. When that happens, most companies want you to try to complete the shop with the other agent and note this in your report.

During an assignment stay alert. You're going to encounter plenty of weird situations that will leave you shaking your head, thinking "How am I going to write THIS up?"

What If the Employee Acts Unprofessionally?

I once walked into a retail store and saw two employees. The one I dealt with was a gentleman, nearly perfect in his presentation. He was kind, friendly, and professional; he tried to up-sell and suggestive-sell. He was did his job well. He wasn't the issue.

His co-worker, a woman, was on the phone the whole time I was there screaming profanity: "Just bring me my money, you M*&^% F*&^%&*, S*&^&* O' B*%&!!!" It was a very uncomfortable situation, and I could tell that the male employee did not know how to respond.

When I wrote my report, all of the questions dealt with the associate I talked to. There wasn't anything that would let me comment on the situation. Remember, companies generally just want what they have listed on the form. If there isn't a space to comment about music, they probably don't need you to comment. I was saved by the very last question: "Would you come back?" I wrote "No!" and proceeded to tell them why.

In a case such as this one, you must remain professional and diplomatic. Use phrases such as "The associate was using inappropriate language for being in the presence of a customer." You'll be able to get your point across without embarrassing the employee too much.

What If the Employee Hits on You?

In one apartment shop, my cover story was that I was single, and looking for a one-bedroom apartment. The leasing agent was a young man who had just moved to the area and had been working at the building for only a few weeks. I doubt that he had much experience within rentals, as we spent a lot of time talking about me. He did a fair job of showing me the community, and the apartment, but never tried to close the deal. Instead, he asked if I had a boyfriend and if I wanted to join him for dinner. I thanked him, but turned him down. He gave me his phone number, and said that he hoped to hear from me.

Writing up this report was hard, because I couldn't help but think of how the young man would feel when his boss eventually approached him. I wrote that he seemed more interested in my personal interests than my needs for the apartment, and although he was very friendly and outgoing, he did not close the deal.

I guess that's true in either case. I didn't go out with him, nor did I get the apartment!

What if You Can't Complete an Assignment?

I know the owner of the shopping company that this situation happened to and I include this story with a blatant, "DON'T DO THIS" warning.

There was a woman who accepted a bowling alley shop, but couldn't complete it, so she *gave it to her husband,* without the consent of the shopping company. DON'T DO THIS!

Her husband took a pal with him to complete the assignment and *they brought the form in with them to the alley.* DON'T DO THIS!

The husband and friend were sitting around, drinking beers, eating nachos, bowling frames, and having a grand old time, when the waitress came up to the table. She saw the husband writing on a form and asked what they were doing. The husband replied, "Oh, We're mystery shoppers! Do you want to see how you did?" He actually showed the waitress her report. Right there, on the spot.

It boggles the mind. DON'T DO THIS!

Needless to say, the woman who originally had accepted the assignment isn't shopping anywhere anytime soon. She passed off a shop, thinking that her husband was competent enough to complete it on his own. She risked the professionalism of the company and pretty much made herself an outcast in the industry. Seriously, DON'T DO THIS!

What If the Building Catches on Fire?

Anything can happen on a shop.

This situation occurred when I was apartment shopping, in a great garden-style community. (A "garden style" is the type of apartments that only go up a few levels, and there are tons of buildings spread throughout the grounds.)

The agent started me out looking at an apartment and was going to tour me around the amenities later. When we came out of the apartment, we saw that the building across the street was on fire! We heard fire engines in the background, and a fairly sizable crowd had gathered to see what was going on. The agent was very professional and excused herself to see if there was anything that she could do.

The community immediately went on "lock-down," and I was held there for about 30 minutes while everything got under control. Thankfully, the family in the apartment was not injured. (Apparently someone had left a curling iron on the stove which was also turned on. The stove melted the curling iron and chaos ensued.) Upon returning to the leasing office, the agent and I completely forgot to tour the community amenities. They were still on lock-down, so the gym, pool, and business center were all closed so there was nothing for me left to do. I described all of this in my report, because being a mystery shopper means that you report events as they occurred. The leasing agent did an excellent job with follow-up, apologizing for the eventful day, and offering another tour if I wanted it. My scheduler told me that I didn't need to go out again, and that I could just write up the report as it happened.

What If the Employee Wants to Save Your Soul?

During a financial shop, I had to meet with an agent about a new savings account. I sat down with the agent, who was very friendly and up-beat, but when I gave her my name, she went into a diatribe about the religious significance and origin.

She went on about what "A good Christian" I must be just because of my name. (For those of you who don't know, "Bethany" was a city near Jerusalem.) I was extremely surprised at her reaction, as it caught me completely off guard. Regardless of my affiliations, this isn't appropriate behavior for any financial institution. I politely told her that I wasn't Christian, and her eyes grew to be the size of dinner plates. My first thought was, "Uh-oh, *now* you've done it!"

She then opened up a whole new can of worms, telling me about her journey to "the Lord" and how she had been saved. She began quoting scripture, and recommended that I go to her church bible-study so that I could learn the "significance of being." Apparently, she told me, my parents were on the right track because they gave me a good name, but it was up to me to realize my path with "the Lord." All I wanted was to open a savings account, and she wanted to save me from the depths of hell.

I successfully managed to redirect her energy to the task at hand, but she kept comparing opening a bank account to opening "your heart to the Lord." She told me that if I prayed a little every day, it was like making "spiritual deposits." Fifteen minutes later, I was able to thank the woman and walk out in complete awe. Of course, I wrote this up as diplomatically as possible, stating that the woman started a religious-based conversation that left me feeling uncomfortable, and she seemed more interested in discussing my spiritual views than opening an account.

What If the Employee Gives Too Much Information?

This report was probably the hardest one I have had to write. An apartment community hired me to evaluate a potential employee who at her current place of employment. They wanted to see what kind of skills she had as an agent before they hired her.

She was fine during the phone presentation and through most of the tour. A few bumps here and there but nothing major. At the close, however, when she brought me back to the office, she got on a tangent about how she was trying to better her life.

She told me that her husband just ran off to Las Vegas with a 19-year-old "hussy" and had left her all alone with no money. She continued telling me about the affair and how she was better off without him, and she began to cry. The agent excused herself for a moment and returned a bit more composed, ready to help me get an apartment. When I told her that I had just begun my search and would not be renting that day, she looked as though she would break down again.

All I said in my report was that she disclosed personal details about her life that were not appropriate for potential renters to hear. As much as I would have loved to refrain from putting anything in the report about it, she was being shopped to see how she dealt with prospects. I really did believe that she was trying to better herself and perhaps this new job would have given her a better income, but I couldn't let my personal views get in the way of the report. Regardless of her situation, she should have kept her personal problems out of the work environment, and certainly not disclose them to potential renters.

As you can see, situations can arise that you may not have even considered! Most assignments will go off without a hitch, but if something strange starts to happen make sure that you maintain your cover story and act with professionalism. In no time you'll gather plenty of your own anecdotes to share around the mystery shopping bon-fire!

Chapter 16

Paying to Shop?

There is a general consensus within the mystery shopping community that shoppers should not have to pay to shop. There is enough information out on the Web that a prospective shopper really can learn the business on their own. It took me about three years before I started compiling all the information I learned about the business, and while I realize that anyone can learn mystery shopping without paying for that information, I also see the value in learning from a professional, rather than just learning by trial and error.

That being said, you **do not** need to spend any more money to learn about mystery shopping. You don't need to pay companies to work for them, you don't need to buy lists of companies, and while getting in a database to receive assignment offers may be useful, a little more time and energy spend on your part could save you the monthly fees. If you're going to pay for anything else, go for the MSPA training, and remember that any money you do spend is tax deductible!

Shopper Fees

Believe it or not, there are mystery shopping companies that actually ask you to pay a fee to work for them. They see it as a way to "distinguish" between people who are serious about shopping and those who are mildly curious. For every one company that charges, there are hundred more that don't ask for payment to be added to their shopper database. These companies are more than happy to increase their shopper listings, thereby filling shops more easily. It is totally up to you if you want to sign on with a company that charges, but I have not seen any worthwhile proof that paying companies will get you more work. In many cases, they may just be scams!

Lists of Mystery Shopping Companies

There are people who compile lists of mystery shopping companies to sell. I've seen these lists being sold on Ebay for $5 up to $499 for a 4 CD Rom set! The problem with most of these lists is that they tend to be outdated. Companies merge and go out of business all the time and the contact information can be invalid. When you see ads about mystery shopping, these lists are usually what people are trying to get you to buy.

Assignment Services

Another way to get your name out there is to pay a monthly or yearly fee to receive mystery shopping assignments. Employers pay nothing for the service. They contact the company providing the service when they have assignments available, and the company then sends out an email to the shoppers in their database. The Assignment company is not a scheduling company. They merely give notice to shoppers when assignments are available. The shoppers pay about $20-$30 a year to receive these emails. There is a bit of controversy regarding these services, so I really recommend checking out the free message boards and signing up with the companies in the back of this book before paying for them.

Certification

If you decide to pay for training or information, I recommend the MSPA certification course. (**www.mysteryshop.org)** The MSPA is a professional organization and is creating an industry standard for mystery shopping.

When you pass the $15 Silver online course, you will receive a certification number that you can post in your applications or provide to companies with which you work. This certification course exists because schedules have to deal with a high "flake" level in new mystery shoppers. It is easier to believe that a shopper is reliable and genuinely interested in working if she takes the time and spends the money to pass certification.

After you pass the silver certification level, you can advance to the Gold level (in-person workshops or a DVD program) These are currently priced at $99. Many schedulers are giving preferential shops to those who are certified, as they recognize the standard of the MSPA. While I believe that certification will assist in receiving more assignments, I don't think that NOT doing it will blackball you from the world of mystery shopping.

There is a huge debate among mystery shoppers whether or not certification is worth it. As someone who has hired shoppers, I can tell you that the MSPA certification number does get you noticed. I hired someone with Gold-level certification to complete some shops for me. She ended up dropping them, so I turned to the folks who had taken my courses and bought this training program, to pick up the slack. Like me, some companies may not care if you have certification, they just want you to get the job done. But, as I mentioned, that Gold certification number did get her noticed. It's a bit of a Catch-22.

I received the following letter when the certification process was just starting. Since that time, the MSPA has created a DVD training course as an alternative to the Gold-level workshops.

From the Desk of Mike Green, MSPA President, 2002

"MSPA SHOPPER CERTIFICATION INFORMATION

The Mystery Shopping Providers Association (MSPA) is pleased to introduce two exciting certification courses for our shoppers worldwide. The MSPA recognizes that mystery shopping is a profession, not just a hobby and that you, the shopper are our most important asset.

As in the case of other professions, we believe that a means of addressing shopper education and certification is necessary. In response to this need, we have developed an on-line Silver Certification program and a more in-depth Gold Certificate program to be offered in person.

Mystery shopping is like any other industry; continuing education is considered an asset to improve your success and to show your commitment to your chosen profession. We would like to invite you to take one if not both of the MSPA certification programs to raise your level of understanding of our industry. Companies are always looking to hire the best and brightest, and this certification is one method of setting you apart.

SILVER CERTIFICATION

This is the first step in a two-step process. The goal of Silver Certification is to confirm that you have the BASIC SKILLS required to be a successful mystery shopper. This is a web-based test, which can be taken on-line by anyone, anywhere. Go to www.mysteryshop.org and look under the Shoppers section for Certification. You can review the basics of mystery shopping, the responsibilities of mystery shoppers, traits of a good mystery shopper and will be provided guidelines on remaining anonymous, observation skills, etc.

You will also be required to read and agree to the MSPA Standards and Ethics Agreement for shoppers, which is very similar to the one that all

MSPA members practice. Once you are finished reading, you will be required to take the 38 question test and pass at least 80% correct.

Note: The questions are randomized and the test is different for each person taking the test. The cost of the Silver Certification test is only $15 and can be paid by credit card. If you pass this test, you will be directed to a website where a certificate (printable) and confirmation number will be issued. In the event that you do not pass, you will be eligible to take the test again in 90 days.

When you pass, please e-mail (DO NOT CALL) the MSPA companies you work with and inform them of your new status. They will need your e-mail address and certification number to confirm your status. You will then also be eligible to sign up for Gold Certification workshop.

GOLD CERTIFICATION

After you have passed the Silver Certification test, you are eligible to attend a Gold Certification Workshop. In 2002, the MSPA debuted our first ever workshop. It was very successful and proved to be in high demand from both shoppers and mystery shopping companies alike. Thus, we have decided to take the in-person workshops nationwide with an aggressive schedule across the US and Canada.

A major highlight of these workshops will be meeting mystery shopping company owners and/or staff members at most seminars. During the workshop, you will experience many opportunities to learn, share and develop your business as an independent contractor.

Gold Certification tells companies who want to hire you that you have been trained in the essentials of mystery shopping and demonstrates you've taken the time and made the effort to become an expert mystery shopper. The Gold Certification Workshop will last 7 hours and will cost $99 per attendee. Please go to http://www.mysteryshop.org/gold.php to sign up for a seminar or to see a list of cities where the classes will be held."

Chapter 17

Scams

Mystery shopping might seem too good to be true, and there are those who will try to take advantage of people trying to get into the field. If anyone tries to tell you that you can make thousands of dollars a month mystery shopping, or receive large ticket items, such as TVs for free, they're trying to con you.

The Newspaper Scam

You've probably seen ads in the paper similar to this:

> Mystery shoppers: Earn $20-$40/hour! Local businesses. FREE merchandise, meals, movies & more! No exp. necessary! www.fictionalwebsite.com 1-800-Shop-More

You might think that you can get a job as a mystery shopper by contacting them, but such is not the case. Most mystery shopping companies do NOT advertise in the paper. If you ever see an ad that deals with mystery shopping, more often than not that company is trying to sell you information about getting started as a mystery shopper. You'll pay $50 or more for their listings and information.

That, in and of itself, is not a scam. There are plenty of people earning a legitimate living by helping others get started in various fields. We're called consultants. I'm one of them, and I'm certainly not a scam!

The ads that you need to watch out for are ones that will direct you to a local number to get information about mystery shopping. That phone number refers you to another number, an 800- or 900-number, which CHARGES you for the phone call. During the recorded message, you will learn that mystery shopping can make you thousands of dollars per month and that you can receive big-ticket items such as TVs for free.

This is all completely false and often leads people to assumed that mystery shopping is a scam! I assure you that it is not. Mystery shopping companies generally don't advertise in the newspaper, so be aware of that when answering any ad. Make sure that the number you are calling has specific information about the services provided or sought and that it doesn't refer you to another phone number. So that you understand the difference, some *merchandising* companies do advertise for jobs in the newspaper usually under "General Help Wanted," but mystery shopping companies don't.

The Bank Scam

All banks get shopped. Some require the use of their customers to perform evaluations, because it is very difficult to try and pretend to close a bank account, if you don't have one there in the first place! Financial institutions are always looking for shoppers in their branches, and from time to time, they may contact their current clients to see if anyone is interested in performing the work.

Scam artists will contact potential shoppers pretending that they are banks looking for shoppers. You may receive an e-mail or regular piece of bulk mail that says you can get paid to be a mystery shopper for your bank. They tell you that all you need to do is provide your name, your bank name, and your bank account number. Sometimes they ask for a Social Security number. DO NOT give out any personal information in an unsolicited request to be a mystery shopper for your bank!

(Remember, legitimate companies will need your SSN to pay you and your routing number for direct deposit.)

Make sure that you check out any unsolicited offer to be a mystery shopper. You can call a different branch of a bank to get the name of the mystery shopping company that holds the account, and verify the company itself through the MSPA or Volition. Make sure that you report any unethical offer to the Better Business Bureau.

Mystery shopping is a legitimate way to earn great extra income, and shoppers need to be aware of the scams in order to keep it a positive experience for all involved.

The Phishing Scam

Some unscrupulous thieves cast a large net over several thousand e-mails trying to get someone to reveal some important information. It could be that they're pretending to be your bank, PayPal, or even a mystery shopping company. This is commonly known as *phishing*. On the next few pages are two examples of phishing scams that I personally received in my.

This e-mail is from "Bank of America." It is concerned with the "unusual number of invalid logins attempts" on my account, and the company wants to verify that I'm really me. It wants me to click on the link to update my account information.

You'll see that the images used are the Bank of America's logo, so the email looks legitimate. The e-mail address even appears to be from Bank of America as well.

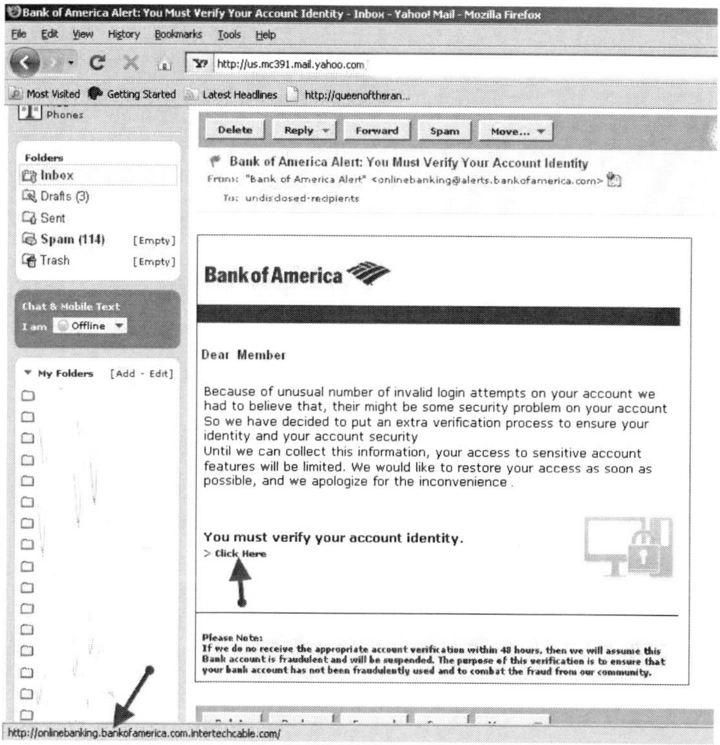

However, when I put my mouse over the link I'm supposed to click on it reveals the actual address I would be heading to as:

http://onlinebanking.bankofamerica.com.intertechcable.com "Onlinebanking," "Bankofamerica," and "com," are all subdomains of the website "intertechcable.com". This means that the real website I'm going to is "intertechcable.com" not Bank of America!

The next example is from PayPal. I received a notice from PayPal telling me that there have been too many logon attempts to my account from a foreign IP address. I am encouraged to update my account as soon as possible.

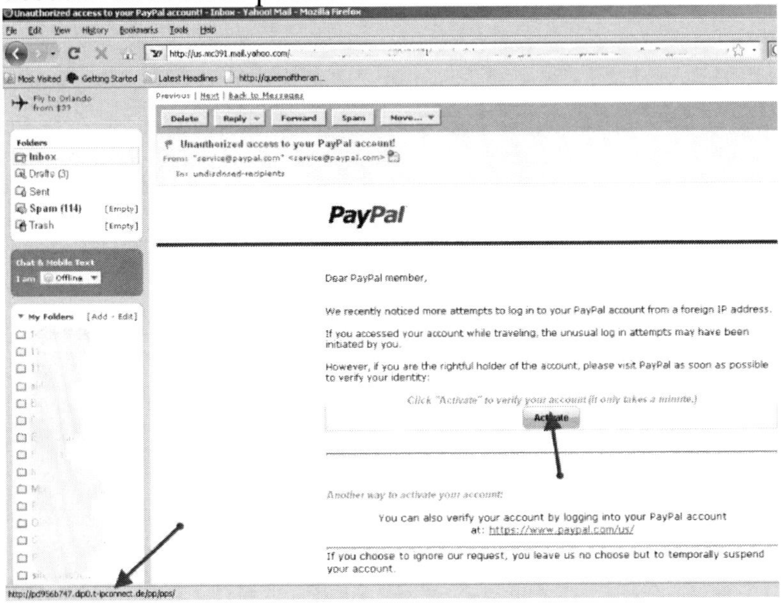

This email looks real as well, since PayPal's logos are used. However, when you mouse over the "activate" button, you see that the link actually goes to:

http://pd956b747.dip0.t-ipconnect.de/pp/pps/

"pd956b747" and "dip0" are subdomains of the website "t-ipconnect.de". You'll be taken to that website not PayPal. The extension on the website (.de) is for Germany. Just like ".com" is for "company" and .net is for "network". There's no way this e-mail is really from PayPal, even though it looks real!

What would happen if you clicked through to the websites offered in these e-mails? You'd see a website that looked just like the one you thought you were supposed to be visiting. Almost anyone can design a website these days, and it's not hard to make a website that looks like Bank of America or PayPal or anything else for that matter.

Once you're at the site, you'll be prompted to login, and thinking it's a real site, you will offer up your user ID and password. In actuality, you have just given your information to a scam artist to use as he sees fit. These scammers send out millions of e-mails each day in hopes that someone will not look clearly at the links and click through to enter their login information.

Welcome to the world of identity theft.

You may be curious as to how mystery shopping companies factor into all of this. Many pay by PayPal or direct deposit through your bank. If some unscrupulous person gets your user ID and password to a mystery shopping company site, he might be able to get your payment processing information. Remember, we're not talking about hackers who break into computers and take information. These phishers contact you, and you unwittingly give out information thinking that they're legitimate.

If a mystery shopping company sends you an e-mail to update your information (and they do from time to time), DO NOT click on ANY link in ANY e-mail! Contact the company through the em-mail address you already have for them to verify they are actually updating their database. You can always login to the company's site to update your info.

Please make sure that you tell any mystery shopping company if you receive any such e-mail. They will want to know that their shoppers are being targeted for phishing scams.

The Certified Check Scam

In the past few years many scams have popped up involving certified checks and mystery shopping

The scam is simple: you'll be asked to mystery shop a Western Union or payday loan business. You receive a check that looks so real that the teller won't even suspect it's a fake. The amount will be enough to cover your "mystery shop" fee and whatever amount the 'shopping company' needs you to send through Western Union. For example, the 'shopping company' may give you a $1,500 check for you to deposit at your bank and evaluate the process. It will say that $500 is your fee, and instruct you to wire the remaining $1,000 through Western Union back to the company. Since the check you received is not good to begin with, you're actually wiring your own $1,000 to the scammer.

Most mystery shops pay $10–$50 each, not $500 and mystery shopping companies DO NOT pay in certified checks. Your payment will either be a traditional check that is sent in the mail or an electronic payment through direct deposit or PayPal. If you ever see an ad for a Mystery Shopper or an assignment that involves wiring money through Western Union, RUN. It's not legitimate!

For more tips on spotting scammers *I Got Scammed, So You Don't Have To!* shows you how to track e-mails and trace IP addresses. It also offers over 300 ideas, resources, and company listings for finding legitimate work at home jobs.

Visit **www.QueenoftheRandomJob.com** for more information.

Chapter 18

Start Your Own Mystery Shopping Company

It's a natural progression to start as a mystery shopper and move on to various roles behind the scenes. Before you make the jump, there are a few issues to consider. .

My mystery shopping company, Shop Incognito, came into being by pure accident. I had been shopping for several years, wrote the first (second and third) versions of this book, had done some scheduling and editing for companies, and was teaching mystery shopping classes in the Detroit area. Because I received a lot of press from the classes, businesses started contacting me to have me train their employees and set up mystery shopping programs for them. It was an amazing learning experience, and after running my own mystery shopping company for two years, I realized it was way too much work for me. I'm more of the free-spirit, random-job type of gal and the work required just took too much of my energy. You, however, may love it, and so I want to give you some insight into my experience, and a launching pad to start your own mystery shopping or scheduling company.

What About Being a Scheduler?

Scheduling companies generally work *with* mystery shopping companies. The mystery shopping company does the marketing and advertising of its services, secures the client, creates the forms, collects the money from the client, pays the shopper, the schedulers, and handles the taxes.

The scheduler is responsible for finding the shoppers, being available for emergencies, rescheduling shops when someone flakes, (or does it incorrectly) giving feedback to the shoppers, and editing the reports.

If scheduling suits your fancy, you can hire yourself out as an independent scheduler to mystery shopping companies. If you get enough clients, you can hire others to work along with you. As a scheduler, you can also work within a scheduling company or a mystery shopping company. Call up the scheduling companies in the back of this book to ask about their hiring procedures. Remember that it is generally frowned upon to work with other mystery shopping companies since most of your focus should be with your main company.

There is no hard and fast rule on whether you should work alone or with others. It really just depends on your own style and what you're looking for. Keep in mind that if you work alone as a scheduler, you'll need to find clients (the mystery shopping companies) just like the mystery shopping has to find clients (the businesses who get shopped). Both require that you learn a little about running your own business, marketing, sales, and tax reporting.

Giving Up Mystery Shopping

The hardest part of starting your own mystery shopping or becoming a scheduler is that you have to give up your life as a Mystery Shopper.

It is a HUGE conflict of interest for you to be securing clients and finding shoppers of your own while keeping your Mystery Shopper status. It is against most confidentially/ICA agreements for you to work at a market research, scheduling, or mystery shopping company as a shopper, and with good reason. Other companies don't want you learning the names of their clients, how much they're paying shoppers, and the types of forms they use so that you can take it for your own business. It is a bit of a transition, but you do have to say goodbye to shopping. Trust me, it's not like it will be the last shop you ever do…you will have shoppers that flake on you, so you'll be doing some emergency shops of your own!

Selecting Your Niche

As a Mystery Shopper, you already know that many different types of assignments are available. As a company owner, you have to decide if there is one in particular type that you want to focus on or if you're open to any industry or type of assignment. You'll need to develop forms for each client. You could start off with a standard template, and then offer to customize for a higher fee.

Here are some target markets to get you started:

Telephone	Internet
Apartment	Retail
Restaurant	Entertainment
Hospitality	Real Estate
Health and wellness	Service businesses
Schools and Daycares	Competition Shops
Focus Groups	Product Testing
Audio Shops	Video Shops
Product Demonstrations	Street Surveys
Fair-Housing and Discrimination	Handicap and Accessibility
Loss-Prevention Issues	Compliance Issues
Merchandising Set-ups	Pre-employment screening

Don't forget that you'll need a shopper database to match your niche market.

- **Students:** Testing procedures, college campus tours, nightclubs.
- **Seniors:** Retirement villas, in-home estimators, insurance companies.
- **Women:** Car dealerships, automotive shops, bridal boutiques.
- **Families:** Day cares, car rentals, schools.
- **Physically Impaired:** Handicap mobility issues.
- **Ethnically Diverse:** Fair housing practices, hiring procedures.
- **Foreign Language Speakers:** Salons, instructional videos.

Issues to Consider

Besides deciding on a corporate structure, taxes, marketing promotions, formulating contracts, and all the normal business issues, there are many items that you need to really think through before starting your own mystery shopping company. The following questions will help you put things in place before you start:

- How will you find shoppers?
- How will you find them in an emergency?
- How are shoppers trained?
- How often do shoppers visit the same location?
- How will you keep track of shopper rotation?
- How are forms sent and submitted?
- How soon do reports get returned from the shopper?
- What is the policy if your shopper gets caught? (from both the shopper and client perspective)
- What is your policy if a shopper lies on the form? (from both the shopper and client perspective)
- How will you monitor your shoppers?
- How will you pay your shoppers?
- What is the schedule for delivering payment?
- How will you keep track of scheduling the shoppers?
- How will you edit forms?
- How soon do reports get returned to the client?
- Will you offer audio/video shops? How will you get the gear to your shoppers? How will you train them to use it? What kind of guarantee will you have for it's return?
- Will you offer to shop the competition?
- Will you offer a free sample shop?

- Will you give discounts to clients for multiple shops, or over a duration of time? (ie: once a month for the next 6 months)
- What kind of a deposit do you need from the client?
- How long does will it take for you to receive the balance?
- Will you have customized or standard forms?

Deciding What to Charge

A lot of people go into business for themselves because they want a higher rate of pay. As your own mystery shopping company, you can set your rates, as well as your shopper rates, to whatever you like! Don't get too excited though. There are hundreds of competitors out there with decades more experience than you, and so you need to make sure that you're priced competitively and have a unique niche.

I highly recommend that you shop some of your competition to see how much they charge and the services they provide to determine your own value positioning. You can certainly pretend that you're a small business owner who wants mystery shopping assignments completed for your establishment. It will be tricky, of course, because the good mystery shopping companies will do research on your business to provide you with ideas and suggestions for your shopping program. If you have friends with small businesses, it will be much easier for you to do this research without completely fabricating a scenario in which you need to have mystery shops performed.

The first mystery shop order Shop Incognito received was priced way below the market rate. (Of course, this is probably why I got the bid!) I had no idea what other mystery shopping companies were charging for their services, and I just guessed based on what I would pay my shoppers and what amount would be worth it to me. In the end, I learned a valuable lesson, and quickly hired small business owners to call various companies and get quotes and sample shops from other mystery shopping companies. That's right…I was the shopper who shopped the companies!

Before you seek out clients, check around your local area to see if the compensation would be worth it to you. Reading some business books and learning the basics about business and administration is imperative for any small business owner as well. You are no longer going to be an independent contractor; you'll be working with several shoppers at once and will need to learn how to effectively manage people. Likewise, you'll be working with company owners and so you'll need to learn negotiation, sales, and marketing techniques as well.

Ideas to Get Started

If you're ready to find some mystery shopping clients of your own, the best way to get started is to talk to small business owners that you already know. Don't bother trying to poach clients from other mystery shopping companies. This is a really small industry and your lack of ethics will soon be known.

You can find small business owners by joining the Chamber of Commerce in your area, logging on to **www.Meetup.com** and finding business groups in your area, and through the social media sites **www.LinkedIn.com** and **www.Biznik.com**. Keep in mind that small business owners may not have the cash-flow to order large shops, but if you can show them the benefits mystery shopping will bring to their business, you might get a few clients.

As an incentive, you can offer a free shop of their location or of a competitor to get them interested and engaged in the process.

After the shop is completed, you can offer training sessions for the employees and tips to help them increase effectiveness.

Some small business owners may have only heard of mystery shopping through radio, TV, or online and believe it's a scam. You may face some preconceived notions regarding the legitimacy of the business. Start collecting articles about the industry that shows it in a positive light. That way, you'll be plenty armed with facts and resources to overcome any objection.

What You Never Realized

It wasn't until I ran my own mystery shopping company that I understood what it meant to be a good shopper. You'd think it would be easy, right? Get an assignment, do the assignment as asked, write up the form and move on your merry way.

As a mystery shopping company owner, I have encountered a shopper who drank too much at a restaurant and couldn't complete the assignment; a shopper who broke her leg on a shop; a shopper who went to the wrong location of a chain store and still demanded to be paid; a shopper with the writing skills of a fourth grader; a shopper who decided to hand write the form even though it was a fillable Word® form; a shopper who said she was Internet savvy but clearly wasn't; and an MSPA Gold-certified mystery shopper who completely flaked on an assignment without apology or remorse. I think her exact words were, "Oops. Oh well."

There *are* thousands of shoppers who are reliable and do good work. Finding them can be a challenge, and once you do, make sure that your pay rates, assignment types, and payment time frames are worth it for them to keep working for you. If you're constantly demanding more from them than other companies, they'll choose not to work for you anymore.

Working with businesses in setting up their programs is a little less stressful. However, chances are that you'll have unreasonable deadlines imposed upon you; companies will ask for verification or guarantee of work (for example, verifying that the shopper didn't fake the form); You may have forms returned to you, you may have to hunt down payment, or the business could decide to change the scope of the project mid-shop. Most of these problems can be averted by having a solid contract in place. Get used to embracing contracts. Collect deposits up front, and make sure that everything you expect of each party is laid out in a clear, concise manner.

The first year of running your business will be the hardest. It will take time to build a reputation and develop your client base. If you love mystery shopping, market research and customer service, you might find that running your own company is just the business opportunity you've been looking for.

Resources

How I Did It!
(My Mystery Shopping Diary)

For several years, I took a hiatus as a shopper while I went "to the other side" to teach others how to get started and avoid scams, as well as to secure a few clients of my own as a mystery shopping company. This led me to an interesting thought: Have I been teaching it for so long that I've really lost touch with what a new shopper goes through?

I made a conscious decision when I started teaching classes, NOT to do any more shops. It just seemed like a conflict of interest. After all, I'd be training my competition! Once I started getting clients of my own, I knew I couldn't shop for other companies anymore. It's a rule of thumb that if you work for a mystery shopping company, you can't shop for other mystery shopping companies.

It had been well over two years since I had my own clients, so I figured I was safe to venture into the world of shopping again. After all, I know those NDAs inside and out, and I had no desire to hurt the very industry that had given me so much over the years.

To make matters more interesting I just moved from Detroit to Seattle. I was unemployed and wasn't interested in finding full-time work. I had the CD Rom for this training program to finish, and didn't want to give the majority of my time to an employer. I had lived in Seattle before, so it wasn't completely foreign, but it certainly had changed since I had lived there last. Would I actually be able to make some money, hopefully enough to live off of for the next few months, just by mystery shopping?

The Internet has really made mystery shopping known, and I was concerned about competition. Yes, I know I talk about "the flake factor" but I also know that schedulers are always looking for good shoppers. Unfortunately for me, (but good for this experiment) there is a LOT of turnover for schedulers, and most of the ones that I had developed rapport with had moved on to various things. I couldn't use my previous contacts to get my foot in the door. As a shopper, I was signed on with over 150 companies. And while I kept track of who was merging and who went out of business, I hadn't really had personal contact with these folks in years. I had to start all over again.

I should mention that when the MSPA first came out with their certification program, I took the silver level quiz, just because I was curious as to what it entailed. So, as my little cheat, I entered my silver certification code into the applications that requested it.

Here is my record of what I did, each day for a month, and the results that it brought.

Day 1

1) Got new e-mail address that I vowed to use specifically for shopping
2) Went to **www.Volition.com** to see what shops were open in my area
3) Applied to the companies that had open shops. I didn't really think I'd get them, but at least I'd be in the company's database for when new shops opened up again.
4) Applied to the main scheduling companies

5) Went to the MSPA site (**www.mysteryshop.org**) to see what companies had open shops in my area, and applied to those companies.

I nearly immediately started getting assignment offers in my e-mail. By the time I was ready to quit for the day, (I'd say it was about 2 hours worth of work) I had applied to 2 mystery shopping companies, 3 scheduling companies, and received my first 2 assignments, (apartments) the first to be completed on Thursday! ($20 each)

Day 2

1) Checked my e-mail
2) Checked Volition again
3) Checked MSPA again
4) Checked the company's that I already applied to, just in case new jobs had appeared
5) Applied to 6 more mystery shopping companies

Most of the companies that I applied to used the SASSIE system, which has a very quick online application. There were a few that required long training and questionnaires, which made me bored and tired, frankly. I vowed that I would sit down at some point and actually do what I recommended: write out my best shopping experience, my worst shopping experience, and my most recent shopping experience, as well as list all the cities that I was willing to shop in, and what made me a good shopper.

By the end of the day, I had only secured one in-person focus group ($75) that I had found from **www.craigslist.com,** in the "etc" job listings. I think Craigslist is a good resource for finding weird, random ways to get some extra cash, but the user really has to be wary about scams. There's a lot of people who are just trying to get your e-mail address to send spam to, or con you out of some money. I did some research on the company before I called them, so I knew that they were legit. I advise anyone to do the same. You can any company that proposes to do market research, focus groups, or surveys up in your local yellow pages. If they're there, chances are they're pretty legit. If they're not, well, its better to be safe than sorry!

Day 3

1) Joined the Shopper's Meeting Network, (**www.mysteryshopsol.com**) just because it sounded like fun
2) Checked my e-mail
3) Checked Volition again
4) Checked MSPA again
5) Checked the job boards of the companies I had already applied to
6) Applied to 6 more mystery shopping companies

I feel like I should note here that the mystery shopping companies that I've been applying to are the ones who have had listings on either MSPA or Volition. There are over 170 companies listed in my book, and I have no desire to go through each and every one and apply to them all this weekend. I wanted to get started QUICKLY, (that American Express bill is coming due soon!) so I've been sticking to the companies that are actively recruiting shoppers in my area right now. The only way to find those is through **Volition.com**, the MSPA site, (**mysteryshop.org**)

Jobslinger.com, and a few random other sites like **craigslist.com** and **wahm.com**, (but I wouldn't recommend them as a first stop) and through the assignment services like **ShadowShopper.com** and **MoneyandShopping.com.** Those charge money, so again, I wouldn't recommend those as a first stop either.

Today, I went on my first shop in 4 years! Wow, was I nervous! It was kinda funny, because I really wanted to do well, so I read and re-read the instructions over and over. It was for an apartment shop that had a target, (which I hate, but apartments pay well) and of course, I got passed off. But all in all, I think I did an ok job at it. I'll hopefully get some feedback soon.

Also today, I decided to go to the MSPA gold certification conference. I was wrestling with this decision, as its $99, and I really wasn't interested in joining the ranks of a consistent shopper. Ideally, I'd just be doing the shopping thing for a few months until my CD was complete, and then start marketing that…also, I'm studying for my Real Estate licensing exam, and so I didn't think that Gold Certification would help me out in the long run. But, I do really believe that we can always learn something new, and I thought it would be good to make contacts with people again. So, begrudgingly, I signed up for it. Luckily for me, it'll be in my area in just 2 weeks, so its not like I have to fly anywhere. I'm curious to see what new things I'll discover.

I secured another apartment shop ($20) to be done this weekend. So, if you're keeping track, in 2 days, I have signed up with 17 companies (schedulers included) and received 3 apartment shops and 1 focus group, for a total of $135.

Day 4

1) Checked my e-mail

2) Checked Volition
3) Checked the job boards on the companies I had already applied to
4) Applied to 5 more MS companies
5) Did my 2nd apartment shop today

At this point, I wished that SASSIE was more universal. It's a pain to have to log into each Mystery Shopping Company's site to view the job board and apply for assignments. But, that's the thing. SASSIE is really just software, it's not a service for shoppers. I think that's what Mystery Shopping Solutions (**www.myshopshol.com**) provides, but I'm not quite sure. I have to look more into them.

Today, I picked up a bank shop ($18) that needs to be done on Monday. Not a big deal, just pretending that I need to open a new account. I don't really like the ones that require you to sign up for a new checking or savings account. I prefer to remain anonymous.

Day 5

I haven't yet heard from my scheduler whether she received my report yesterday, and frankly, I'm a bit paranoid. I know that there is the strict "24-hour" turnover rule, and I wanted to be sure that she got it, but I don't know if she works on the weekends. Just to be sure, I sent a follow-up e-mail.

Today, I really didn't feel like going through the company listings. I had one shop that I needed to complete, (my 3rd apartment) and I just picked up an oil change ($10 payment, $20 reimbursement) for tomorrow. Usually I don't do reimbursement shops like restaurants, because I prefer getting paid, as opposed to just getting compensated. But, I really needed an oil change! I just drove from Detroit to Seattle, and I haven't had an oil change since I got here, so it was a welcomed surprise when I saw that one open!

All I have lined up for next week is the oil change and bank shop for Monday, and the focus group on Wednesday. I'm having mixed feelings about this experience so far. On the one hand, I'm pretty impressed that within 5 days, I have made $153 from mystery shopping. Of course, I'm not going to see that money for another month, but it's definitely a start. If you think about it, the fees have covered both the silver and gold certification costs as well as nearly covering the cost of one copy of The Mystery Shopper CD Rom. From a new shopper's point of view, I would have felt the costs were reasonable for those products based on how quickly I could make the money back.

On the other hand, when I was a shopper before, I was pulling in $1500+ a month. And, that kind of money would really be useful right now. Especially because I think I'm going to devote most of my energy to mystery shopping. I'm trying to remind myself that I'm starting over. After all, the first month that I did mystery shopping, way back in 1999, I only did that one shop. So far, I have 6 secured in 5 days. We'll have to see what next week brings.

At this point, though, I'm seriously considering getting a digital camera. There is one company in particular that needs field auditors to take pictures of the outside of buildings. The pay isn't that great, but that's all they need. Just pictures. So, I'm thinking about it. The main question comes down to: am I desperate enough for money that I'll take ANY kind of assignment that comes my way?

I'm not a fan of merchandising. I've only done a few of those, and they were long, boring and hard. I have no idea what a Plan-o-gram is, nor do I really care to…but, at the moment, I need money, and I don't want to get a job. I think I'll probably see how this week goes and debate it later. Which reminds me, though, I haven't yet checked out **www.Narms.com** to see what's going on in the Merchandising world. They're a great site because they allow people to post profiles too.

How much of an experiment do I want to turn this into? Am I willing to go out and do product demonstrations? Field Surveys? All those things I really hate doing? I've done temp-type work before...I remember helping out at a national company's sales event, where all I had to do is return clothing from the dressing room to the floor. That was hard only because I had to wear heels the whole time. I'm more of a sandals kind of gal. I also remember doing inventory for another large department store. In jewelry, actually. All we had to do was count the number of necklaces and earrings, and whatever else they told us to do. It wasn't hard, but I don't know that I really want to spend my time doing it.

Mostly, I guess, I'm just looking for a way to pay the bills while I'm getting my real estate license, getting the Mystery Shopping CD Rom completed, and deciding what I really want to do with **www.QueenoftheRandomJob.com**.

Just as I'm ready to log off for the evening, I get an e-mail to do a bus depot shop. ($16) I figure, what the heck? I haven't done those before...within 4 minutes, I get a confirmation. Not bad.

Day 6

Oh what a busy day! First of all, I was having printer issues, which wasn't fun. But once that was settled, I went out on my day of shopping. The first stop was the bus depot, and then to get my oil changed, and then to the bank. The oil change was interesting, and I really needed one. Once I got home and looked at the receipt, the coupon wasn't taken into consideration, so I'm wondering what to do next. I just e-mailed my scheduler, so we'll see what happens. As a shopper, I hope this doesn't invalidate the shop, but as a customer, I'm kind of annoyed, and frankly I want to go back there to see what happened. Did they give me the service I requested or not?

(By the way, I did finally receive a confirmation e-mail noting that my apartment shops were received…whew)

While I was in-between shops, I got another call to do credit union shops. So, I took all of those too. They paid $10 each, but if I did them this week, I'd get $15 per shop. I have to do 8, which totals $120. I came home to write up the shops, and then got another offer to do an emergency fitness store. ($15) I also applied for a weight-loss center ($18.) I've never done that one either, so hopefully I'll get it.

I'm getting a bit overwhelmed already, and I haven't even been doing this a week! I set up a dry erase board near my computer which states PENDING shops, ACCEPTED shops, FOLLOW-UP (for those that require follow up, like apartments) and CONFIRMED, so I know that the company received them. I'm also going to start listing the companies that use SASSIE or have Job Boards on the wall too…it's just easier than trying to go through the book, I think. I've been debating maybe creating a list like that as well for the mystery shopping book, but since each company has different locations, I don't know that it would be that beneficial. I think it would be easier if a new shopper did a LITTLE bit of research on their own area.

Now that I've taken some time to reorganize my shops and figure out my schedule for this week, I've reached an interesting conclusion. In 6 days, doing nothing more than applying at 4-5 company's sites a day, and checking the message boards, I have secured 1 focus group and 16 shops totaling $337. If I can keep it up at this rate, I'll have no problem making over $1000 a month...which is all I really need right now to survive. Granted, I would like to pay off some bills too...

One thing that I've found to be helpful is to create folders for each company. At first I thought that I'd do it by whoever assigned the shop, but since it's the company that pays me, not the scheduler, I think it's better to do it that way.

Day 7

I'm getting a little overwhelmed, actually. All these shops are flying at me. I just picked up a weight loss centre shop ($18) that I'll be doing on Thursday. It's a little bit out of my way, but since I have 3 shops in that area, I think it's justified.

I still haven't heard back from my scheduler yet about what to do with the Oil Change shop. And the credit union shops I'm doing are a pain. I have to look for all of this signage, and if its not there, I have to ask an employee where it's posted, and if they say they don't have it posted, I have to ask WHY they don't have it posted. Yeah, they won't peg me as a shopper at ALL. Not a bit. (insert rolling of the eyes here). Not only that, it's a handwritten form, which I have to call in first. So, I have to spend time on the phone calling in my answers, then I have to write out the form and send it in. Thank goodness these pay a bonus because I wouldn't do them at the rate they're usually offered at.

So today was a pretty easy day. All I did was one credit union shop and a home fitness store. Tomorrow is all about banking. One bank and two credit unions, and then I have the focus group at 2pm.

At some point I need to sit down and figure out how all of these things are invoiced. I figure at the end of the month I can send out invoices and such. I just need some consistency…all these companies requiring all of these different little things. Understandable, but annoying.

Day 8

I'm actually really surprised that I haven't heard back from my scheduler about the Oil Change Shop yet. Kind of annoyed, actually.

Well, regardless, today was a pretty easy day. I had 2 credit union shops, and then the focus group, which, lucky for me, didn't require my presence! That's the wonderful thing about focus groups…if they overbook, you still get paid! So, I got $75 just for hanging out in a waiting room for 30 minutes. After that, I did a bank shop, and I got a phone call for 2 apartment shops this weekend, and an acceptance of a Jewelry store. I put in my initial call to the weight loss shop.

Whew.

Surprisingly, I still have time for a social life. I've been hanging out with people in the evening, finishing up most of my shop stuff by 5 or so. Right now I'm trying to figure out how to be more organized. I think the best thing to do is create hanging folders for each day of the week, and put assignments in that need to be done that day. The reason for this, is well, frankly, I almost forgot to call the weight loss centre, which requires a phone a minimum of 24 hours ahead of the onsite visit. Oops. I almost messed that up. So, if I have folders for every day, I can put those that require preliminary calls ahead of time, (some apartments do this too) in the day before its due, and I can go over each assignment at night. I think that may be best.

Another thing that I'm starting to do is put the assignment ID with each shop. For me, obviously, its easier to refer to the shop by name or location, but the companies refer to it by ID number…so it makes sense to keep track of them that way as well for follow up questions and comments.

I haven't gotten a PO box yet though. Should I? I'm only planning on staying in my location for 6 months or so…I would actually like to buy a house instead of rent. I don't know. But it's also making me wonder how long I'm going to keep up this MS thing. Right now, it's just an experiment, and a quick way to make some cash since I'm new in town.

My first 7 days of shopping: I signed up with 22 companies, received way too many job offers, secured 22 shops, and have potentially earned $486. I say "potentially" because we never know if something goes awry and if I won't get paid. It's hard for me to break it up hourly, because I tend to shop in-between living my life. But daily, it works out to $69.43/day. Not bad. I certainly don't feel like I've been working a full 8 hour day. Maybe 4 or 5 at most. At 5 hours/day, it's $13.89 per hour. Not bad…Of course, I really don't count the reading of assignments, etc. It's like a teacher who still has to grade homework and tests at home.

So, lets see…tomorrow I have 2 credit union shops, a weight loss shop, and a jewelry shop. The credit union shops are going a lot quicker than at first, which I'm really glad. On Friday, I have 3 credit union shops, an apartment shop, and an apartment phone shop. I don't have a lot going on for the weekend, though. Just a shop on Saturday. I got an offer to do a price audit next Wednesday. It pays $60 for 5 hours, so I'm going to hopefully get that tomorrow.

Day 9

Wow. Am I tired. Today I really just wished I could stay in bed. But, there's shopping to be done. Today, I got a phone call to do a movie theatre check for tomorrow, but I'm completely booked up! It's too bad too, those checks are fairly easy. All you have to do is count the number of people coming in and out of a movie over a period of a few hours. But, I just can't do it.

Also today I did my weight-loss clinic, which was an interesting experience. I was there for nearly 2 hours. TWO HOURS. And, actually, it was fun, just because I really liked the consultant, but by the time I got home and wrote up the expansive form, I found that I had made less than minimum wage on that job. Definitely not worth the time or effort I put into it.

I decided not to do the jewelry shop today, because I was just too tired. It's not due until the 20th, and I didn't promise a specific day for submission, so I have a few days to complete it. But now…to bed!

Day 10

Still wondering how next week is going to shape up. So far, all I have confirmed is that pricing check for Wednesday. I'm up to $498, not bad…but I need more. I suppose this weekend I should sign up for some more companies. I hate that I have to re-register with all of the ones that I shopped for years ago, but such is the life. Technology improves, databases get installed, and information gets lost.

I finished up my credit union shops, which is good. They were easy enough, but after doing 8, I'm ready to move on. My scheduler was trying to convince me to do another type of assignment that they needed done, but it didn't pay enough and was too far.

I wanted to do an apartment shop today, but my target moved me to Monday. Oi. And this other target at another community isn't picking up the phone! While I love apartment shops, I hate targeted shops. Such a waste of my time. So…if ever I get this target on the phone, hopefully I can set something up for tomorrow. I have that jewelry shop to complete, and I just picked up a retail store that's in that area too.

I finally received an e-mail from my scheduler about the oil change shop, and she said that the client says I shouldn't go back to the location and see if I got what I paid for. This is annoying for several reasons: 1) I want to know if my tires were rotated 2) I want payment for the coupon and 3) how can I prove to the company that I really did what was asked on the shop?

Whatever. Their decision.

Day 11

Could I already be getting burned out on shopping? I'm just so tired…it could also be because I haven't really taken the time to make some decent meals this week. Or, that I haven't worked out at ALL. Come to think of it, I haven't worked out since I got here. Maybe that's where the energy has gone.

So, today, I had an apartment shop, an automotive retail store, and a jewelry store. I also went through all of my files to make sure that I have copies of the shops I did this week, and that all follow-up work has been completed, and that the things I need to mail back to the companies have been organized.

What a good shopper I am.

It's probably time to start signing up with more companies. I haven't gotten more offers this week...actually, that's not true. The offers I've been getting are either 1) too far away 2) I just did the shop last week, (someone probably cancelled) or 3) they don't pay enough for me. It's kind of surprising that retail shops have dropped to a below $10 payscale. A lot are just $5-$7, but the forms are still long-ish.

Actually, what I'm noticing is that there are more "limited fields" in forms than there used to be. This annoys me. I like writing. I can type nearly 80 WPM, and I prefer being able to use descriptive language, rather than be limited by only 150 characters. Seriously. Who can give a good commentary in 150 characters?

Day 12

Today, I took the day off of shopping. I didn't apply anywhere, I didn't do anything. I just spent the day being domestic and caught up on chores. But, no mystery shopping.

Day 13

I can't believe that I haven't written in the past 4 days. It's kinda funny, because I really don't know where the time went! On Monday, I did an apartment shop, and yesterday, I did a pricing shop, where I had to go around different locations and get prices on various grocery items and electronics. Technically, I think it's an audit, but I'm not sure. It was a pain, that's for sure...only because I didn't have a clear plan on where to go, and I didn't get the form until yesterday morning. But, I got it done. If I need to do something like that again, I'll have a much better game plan.

I have been offered lots of shops...but I haven't really been in the mood to take them. The one exception are the 2 financial shops that I need to schedule for next week. Other than that, I haven't really felt the need to find more assignments. I'm up to $545…and I actually could have done a LOT of apartment shops, but the company that does them uses handwritten forms, which are a PAIN, and I really don't want to deal with that right now. I type over 80 WPM…my handwriting is crap. I'm surprised that they're so archaic still. It's a pretty big company.

This weekend is the MSPA Gold conference. I'm looking forward to it actually, because I'm curious to learn what I don't already know. And, of course, there's the schmoozing factor. Getting my name out there to the companies in hopes that my mystery shopping CD might just pique their interest. That's another thing I'm going to be working on next week. The re-record of the CD. And…other stuff too…

Right now though, I'm in a bit of a funk. I'm just not in the mood to do anything. I think I might just head to bed.

Day 15

Today was the MSPA conference…I am now officially GOLD certified! I am so glad that I went…I knew I would be, as there is always a chance to learn something new.

An interesting thing that came up is the concept of violating confidentiality agreements, simply by stating that a business gets shopped. I honestly think that some mystery shopping companies vary with this. I know for certain we're not allowed to say, "who shops who" but I think it varies with companies whether they allow you to talk about the clients, outside of the MS company reference. I'll be interested to see what kind of feedback I get when I send out the CD's.

Overall, it definitely was money worth spent. I got to see some of the company owners that I used to work for years ago, and the fact that they actually remembered my name was quite flattering. I know, it's unique, but still…it's a nice thing.

Day 16

Today I received 3 bank shops for September, ($18/each) and I got a corporate event planning location ($20.) I haven't quite figured out how to phrase that better. Basically, I'm just going in and pretending that I want to book an event at their location. The icing on the cake was for a Mortgage Shop. It's a bit out of my way, but it pays $28 for the phone call and $35 for the onsite visit, PLUS another $10 reimbursement for gas. Not a bad shop.

I need to get a PO Box, and a new phone number. I haven't really applied to any new companies, and I need to get settled into some sort of a routine.

Oi.

Day 24

I haven't written in awhile, and things have not quite taken off. So far, for next month, I have 3 bank shops, the corporate planning shop, the mortgage shop, and a cell phone shop, (which, I might add, I got conned into) totaling $147. That's not a lot. I'd really like to get more assignments, so I spent today going through and applying to more companies. I did get a local cell phone number and PO box, so those things are updated. Officially, I am now signed up with 55 companies…I factored schedulers into that because I want to.

About the cell phone shop…I hate it when schedulers call me, because I feel so guilty about saying no. They always launch into the shop description, when all I really care about it where it's located and how much they're going to pay. So after 5 minutes on the phone with this scheduler explaining the minute details of the shop, she finally asks me if I'd like to do it…I told her that all I really needed to know is where it was located, and how much it paid. She told me, and I tried to turn her down gently, but apparently she was having a really hard time filling the shop. So I agreed. Damn. I'm too nice.

Of course, then she sent over the form, which is 5 pages complete with narratives, and she told me I had to go over the form with her before I did the shop to make sure I understood it.

I know that schedulers have to deal with flaky shoppers not following directions, but I'm getting tired of having to spend my time and my cell phone minutes on the line going over every single line of the shop:

"Ok, now on question one, it asks for the employee's name…that means you need to put the employee's name in that slot. The next question asks for the date and time you were in the store, so you need to put the exact date and time you were in the store. Don't confuse that with the "day" because that would be the day of the week…understand?"

But, I guess this is what a new shopper needs to go through to prove themselves.

Lately, I've been signing up with a lot of companies that require training…I have to go through pages and pages of information, and then do quizzes at the end. I'm proud to say, actually, that I've been getting 100% on these quizzes. But it's still a pain.

Even a company that I did a lot of work for "back in the day" has revamped its application procedure…I have to do a sample shop, as well as submit documentation that I'm an independent contractor. What's up with that?

I guess I'm just tired at this point…So far, for next month I only have $147 worth of shops scheduled. I'd like to get up around $1000.

Day 30!

Exactly one month ago today, I started signing up for assignments. Since that time, I have secured $1381.61 worth of assignments. I have been paid for $213 of those assignments (checks already received and cashed.) I get, on average, 5-10 offers a day…this includes e-mail contact as well as phone. Actually, that's not too bad. It's not my all-time record of $1800-ish, but I'm still not signed up with all the companies that I was working for before. Not only that, I'm still having problems with one company receiving my W-9. I faxed it, I e-mailed it, and I'm a little concerned that it's been lost. I'm really kind of annoyed too, because this company has a TON of apartment shops in my area, and I really want to take them. They still use handwritten forms, which is a pain, but they pay pretty well, so I'm willing to overlook it for awhile. If, that is, I ever get to work for them.

This little experiment has definitely opened my eyes to what a new shopper goes through. It's nice to know that by following my own advice, people really can make money at mystery shopping. It does take some time, at the beginning especially, but after only a month, I have over $1300 worth of shops!

What's even more interesting, is that I have forgotten how important it is to be organized. I have calendars and file folders, and dry-erase boards, plus my own little Xcel file to keep track of things. It would be nice to be able to combine all of this into some sort of system…a one-stop program, so to speak, so that I know when companies need to be invoiced, when follow-up is needed, and making sure that I've been paid. Maybe that's another project down the line.

But for now, I have some shops to finish!

Post Diary Notes:

I just wanted to mention that after I did this little experiment, I went on to surpass my all-time record of earning $1800 in a month. My new current record is $2200!

In addition, that little idea about a scheduling program is what gave birth to TRIBEStrack™, a comprehensive scheduling and accounting software system for independent contractors. You can learn more about it at **www.TRIBEStrack.com**.

I hope that this little exercise gave you some insight into what a new shopper goes through, and shows you that it's not that hard to get started in mystery shopping. You just need to get out there and do it!

Glossary

Audit: A type of Market Research Assignment for verifying certain types of information about a company, such as counting the number of patrons, or checking specific sales signage.

Benefit: A benefit is a feature that would suit the customer's need (for example, if a swimming pool is mentioned because someone liked to swim, or a walk-in closet is shown because someone wanted a lot of storage space).

Client: The company that calls upon a mystery shopping company to perform assignments. Clients include retail stores, banks, apartment buildings, self-storage facilities, and more.

Competitive Shop: Shops completed for the sole purpose of rating competition within the same industry.

Cover Story: The scenario a shopper comes up with to give validity to a shop (for example, when in a retail store, telling an associate that you're looking for a gift for your nephew. In an apartment, coming up with a reason why you are moving, where you are working, and the type of apartment that you need).

Dropped Shop: When a shopper neglects to do an assignment, with or without notice it is called a "dropped shop." This is also referred to as "flaking" on a shop.

Emergency Shop: Assignments that have an impending due date, without having someone to complete them.

Exit Interview/Survey: A type of Market Research that requires an individual to seek one-on-one opinions from patrons regarding customer service directly following their time in a store.

Fair Housing Laws: Rules and regulations in the United States which state that discrimination on the basis of race, color, national origin, religion, sex, familial status, and/or disability is illegal. State and local laws often extend these protected classes to include other characteristics such as sexual preference, age, and student status. In regard to mystery shopping, this would come into play mainly in Real Estate shops, to be sure that the leasing agent isn't discriminating against the shopper or providing information about the types of current residents.

Feature: An aspect of a product or service. In an apartment community, features may include a tanning bed, swimming pool, hot tub, work-out facility, outdoor barbeque area, and so on.

Focus Group/Forum: A type of Market Research where people give their opinion, either in a group, or individually about products, services, or ad campaigns.

Getting Caught: A shopper's worst nightmare. When an employee of an establishment recognizes that the person who is acting as a customer isn't really a customer and that they are only present to evaluate the business and customer service. This usually results in the shop becoming invalid and the shopper not being paid.

Independent Contractor Agreement (ICA): This agreement states that a shopper will not divulge any information he or she learns about a company, its employees, its services or anything else before, after, or during the course of the assignment. This agreement also states that the shopper understands that she is not an employee and will not receive any benefits or Workers Compensation and is responsible for reporting all income earned.

Integrity/Security Shops: Assignments performed for the sole purpose of checking on the honesty of the employees and evaluating a business's loss prevention program. They also revolve around "compliance" issues with regard to underage shoppers buying alcohol and tobacco products.

Merchandising: The act of going into an establishment to stock, refill, or inventory merchandise.

Mock Trial: A practice trial of a judicial case to gauge the opinion of a sample jury.

Mystery Shopper/Auditor/Secret Shopper: Common terms used for someone who gets paid to rate and evaluate aspects of a business by posing as a regular customer.

Mystery Shopping Company: The business that has been hired by its client to complete evaluations on the client's stores, restaurants, entertainment venues, and other services. The mystery shopping company is responsible for creating forms and guidelines for an assignment and recruiting mystery shoppers.

Prophet: An online data-reporting system that some mystery shopping companies use for shoppers to enter their forms online instead of through e-mail, fax, or snail mail. Mystery shopping companies will let you know if you will be using the Prophet system to report your shops.

Reward/Revealing Shop: When a mystery shopper evaluates certain procedures of an establishment, and informs the employee after the fact whether he had followed the guidelines. The employee receives a "reward" from the shopper, after the shopper has "revealed" her true purpose.

SASSIE (Scheduler and Shopper Survey Internet Engine): An online reporting system that some companies use for shoppers to apply and submit forms. If a mystery shopping company uses SASSIE, they will let you know if you will use it to apply for shops through the SASSIE system.

Scheduler: The person in a mystery shopping or scheduling company that has been directed to assign evaluations to mystery shoppers. This person also acts as a contact for shoppers while they are in the process of completing an assignment for questions, comments, or concerns.

Shop: An assignment given to a shopper to evaluate a company's service, products, employees, or store conditions.

Suggestive Selling: Offering other products to go with ones that you have selected (for example, "We have some lovely socks that would go with that outfit," or "Would you like Fries with that?").

Target: The person that the shopper is assigned to evaluate during the course of the shop.

TRIBEStrack™: A scheduling system developed to help mystery shoppers and independent contractors keep track of their business. The acromnym stands for, "Tracking and Reporting for Independent contractors, Business owners, Entrepreneurs, and Solopreneurs". It combines accounting software with scheduling software for a robust, comprehensive program uniquely designed for non-traditional and independent workers. You can learn more at **www.TRIBEStrack.com**.

Up-sell: When an employee recommends a higher grade of a product that you have requested (for example, instead of just serving a rum and coke, asking if you would like a Bacardi ® and coke).

Company Listings

Many people are so eager to get started that they skip right to this section of the book. I'm hoping that you've actually gone through the program so that you know how to conduct yourself as a professional mystery shopper. Unfortunately, many people have been banned from companies due to their unprofessionalism! Before you apply to be a mystery shopper, make sure you know what is expected of you. I have provided over 170 companies and resources to get you started. Below is how the listings are set up:

Company Name	*Company Website*
Company Address	*Twitter*
City/State/Zip	*Facebook*
ID:	*Password:*
Notes:	

You'll notice that the company name, address, website and phone number are listed. In addition, if the company has a Twitter or Facebook page, they are listed as well. At the bottom of the listing, there is a place for you to put your shopper ID and password to log into their sites, and any notes that you wish to write down (for example, when you applied, or the types of assignments that the company does).

The Inevitable Disclaimers

I try extremely hard to keep all of this information current, and constantly look for new, reputable companies to share. It is common for companies to merge, expand to new locations, or go out of business. I ask you to keep this in mind should you find any discrepancy with this list.

Going through this program does not automatically guarantee employment with any company. You have been given the tools and information to succeed, along with a list of companies that are looking for people to fill assignments. If you conduct yourself in a professional manner and treat your employers with respect and courtesy, you will undoubtedly have great success.

When contacting these companies, remember that where they are located does not affect where they perform shops. Target™, Sears™, Subway™, and other large name corporations are located nationwide, if not internationally. The mystery shopping company that is conducting their assignments could be located anywhere. Start by finding those companies that have assignments in your area, even if the company itself isn't physically near you. You can find these companies quickly by starting with the MSPA job board, (**www.mysteryshop.org**) the Volition job board (**www.volition.com**), and **JobSlinger.com**. Pick a few of the scheduling companies to sign up with as well. The scheduling companies have several mystery shopping companies as clients, so you'll be offered a wide array of assignments.

Pick 5-8 companies to start with, and add more companies as you gain confidence. Believe me, I didn't sign on with 150 companies in one afternoon! It takes time, but if you start with the largest pool (the message boards and scheduling companies) you'll be able to get started quickly!

Most importantly, don't forget to have fun!

A&A Merchandising Ltd
3250 Lakeshore Blvd W
Toronto, ONT Can M8V 1M1
ID:
Notes:

www.aamerch.com
T:
FB:
Password:

About Face
2870 Peachtree Rd #292
Atlanta, GA 30305
ID:
Notes:

www.aboutfacecorp.com
T:
FB:
Password:

A Closer Look
460 S. Peachtree NW
Norcross, GA 30071
ID:
Notes:

www.a-closer-look.com
T:
FB:
Password:

ALCOPS
5750 W 95th St Ste #320
Overland Park, KS 66202
ID:
Notes:

www.alcops.com
T:
FB:
Password:

A Customer's Point of View
1555 Pennsylvania Ave
McDonough, GA 30253
ID:
Notes:

www.acpview.com
T:
FB:
Password:

Amusement Advantage
12650 W 64th Ave #E-426
Arvada, CO 80004
ID:
Notes:

www.amusementadvantage.com
T: amuseadvantage
FB:
Password:

Ann Michaels and Associates
3108 S Rt 59
Naperville, IL 60564
ID:
Notes:

www.ishopforyou.com
T:
FB: annmichaelsandassociates
Password:

Anonymous Insights
PO Box 1548
Dublin, OH 43017
ID:
Notes:

www.a-insights.com
T:
FB:
Password:

Apollo Services
921 Transport Way Ste 30
Petaluma, CA 94954
ID:
Notes:

www.ApolloServices.org
T:
FB:
Password:

AQ Services
Asia, Europe, UK
China, Japan
ID:
Notes:

www.aqservices.com
T: aqservices
FB: aqservices
Password:

Ardent Services
6883 South Owens Street
Littleton, CO 80127
ID:
Notes:

www.ardentservices.com
T:
FB:
Password:

Associate Consumer Evals (ACE)
4901 S Limit
Sedalia, Missouri 65301
ID:
Notes:

www.acemysteryshopping.com
T:
FB:
Password:

A Step Above Service Evals
65643 20th Ave N
St Petersburg, Fl 33710
ID:
Notes:

www.serviceevaluations.com
T:
FB:
Password:

Ath Power Consulting
12 Essex St
Andover, MA 01810
ID:
Notes:

www.athpoweronline.com
T:
FB:
Password:

A Top Shop
5353 W Dartmouth Ave Ste 401
Denver, CO 80227
ID:
Notes:

www.atopshop.com
T:
FB:
Password:

At Your Service Marketing
PO Box 7
Chico, TX 76431
ID:
Notes:

www.aysm.com
T:
FB:
Password:

Bare Associates International
US, China, Europe, Middle East
South America
ID:
Notes:

www.bareinternational.com
T:
FB:
Password:

B Business Solutions Inc
55 Greystone Dr
Mountaintop, PA 18707
ID:
Notes:

www.bizshoptalk.com
T:
FB:
Password:

Best Market Audits (BMA)
214 Bridge St
Phoenixville, PA 19460
ID:
Notes:

www.mystery-shopping.com
T:
FB:
Password:

Bestmark Mystery Shopping Co
5605 Green Circle Dr Ste #200
Minnetonka, MN 55343
ID:
Notes:

www.bestmark.com
T:
FB:
Password:

Beyond Hello
PO Box 5240
Madison, WI 53705
ID:
Notes:

www.beyondhello.com
T: beyond hello
FB: yes~ search their name
Password:

Beyond Marketing Group
PO Box 1344
Winston-Salem, NC 27116
ID:
Notes:

www.beyondmarketinggroup.com
T:
FB:
Password:

Business Evaluation Services
POB 20907
Bakersfield, CA 93390
ID:
Notes:

www.mysteryshopperservices.com
T:
FB:
Password:

Business Insights Group
115 Stone Quarry Rd Ste 220
Monaca, PA 15061
ID:
Notes:

www.businessinsights.com
T:
FB:
Password:

Business Research Lab
397 River St
Chester, VT 05143
ID:
Notes:

www.busreslab.com
T:
FB:
Password:

Campus Consulting
US/Canada

ID:
Notes:

www.shopaudits.com
T:
FB:
Password:

Capstone Research
695 Rte 46 W
Fairfield, NJ 07004
ID:
Notes:

www.capstoneresearch.com
T:
FB:
Password:

Checkmark Inc
PO Box 11595
Zephyr Cove, NV 89448
ID:
Notes:

www.checkmarkinc.com
T:
FB:
Password:

Check Up Marketing
300 Perimeter Pk Dr Ste D
Morrisville, NC 27560
ID:
Notes:

www.checkupmarketing.com
T:
FB:
Password:

CKA Group
4950 C York Rd #236 POB 2000T:
Buckingham, PA 18912
ID:
Notes:

www.ckagroup.com

FB:
Password:

Concerto
220 Cambie Street Ste 400
Vancouver BC V6B 2M9
ID:
Notes:

www.sensusshop.com
T:
FB:
Password:

Confero
1152 Executive Circle
Cary, NC 27511
ID:
Notes:

www.conferoinc.com
T: confero
FB: confer
Password:

Consumer Connection
PO Box 691
Sechelt, BC CAN V0N 3A0
ID:
Notes:

www.consumerconnection.net
T:
FB:
Password:

Consumer Impressions Inc
PO Box 866996
Plano, TX 75086
ID:
Notes:

www.consumerimpressions.com
T:
FB:
Password:

Corporate Intelligence Group
6438 LaPosta Dr
El Paso, TX 79912
ID:
Notes:

www.mysteryshoppers.com
T:
FB:
Password:

Corporate Research Int'll
613 S Main St
Findlay, OH 45840
ID:
Notes:

www.mysteryshops.com
T:
FB:
Password:

Count On Us
2250 Sherman Ave A-4
Pennsauken, NJ 08110
ID:
Notes:

www.ucountonus.com
T:
FB:
Password:

Coyle Hospitality Group
224 Madison Ave #369
New York, NY 10016
ID:
Notes:

www.coylehospitality.com
T: coyleexperience
FB: coylehospitality
Password:

Creative Image Associates Inc
603 Mass Ave
Lunenburg, MA 01462
ID:
Notes:

www.creativeimage.net
T:
FB:
Password:

Creative Marketing Concepts
1321 Duke St Ste 305
Alexandria, VA 22314
ID:
Notes:

www.getcreativemarketing.com
T:
FB:
Password:

Creative Marketing Concepts
1321 Duke St Ste 305
Alexandria, VA 22314
ID:
Notes:

www.getcreativemarketing.com
T:
FB:
Password:

CRG Mystery Shoppers
no address given

ID:
Notes:

www.CRG2000.com
T:
FB:
Password:

Customer 1st/1st Point Resources
225 Commerce Place
Greensboro, NC 27401
ID:
Notes:

www.customer-1st.com
T:
FB:
Password:

Customerize
9921 Carmel Mt Rd, Ste 185
San Diego, CA 92129
ID:
Notes:

www.customerize.com
T:
FB:
Password:

Customer Perspectives
213 W River Road
Hooksett, NH 03106
ID:
Notes:

www.customerperspectives.com
T:
FB:
Password:

Customer Service Experts
2901 Riva Trace Parkway Ste 100
Annapolis, MD 21401
ID:
Notes:

www.customerserviceexperts.com
T:
FB:
Password:

Customer Service Perceptions
Lookout Mountain, TN 37350

ID:
Notes:

www.csperceptions.com
T:
FB:
Password:

Customer Service Profiles
12020 Shamrock Plaza Ste 310
Omaha, NE
ID:
Notes:

www.csprofiles.com
T:
FB:
Password:

Data Quest Investigations, LTD
896 Beacon Street
Boston, MASS 02215
ID:
Notes:

www.dataquestonline.com
T:
FB:
Password:

David Sparks and Associates
107 Clemson St
Clemson, SC 29631
ID:
Notes:

www.sparksresearch.com
T:
FB:
Password:

Delve
11971 Westline Industrial Dr #200
St Louis, MO 63146
ID:
Notes:

www.delve.com
T:
FB:
Password:

Devon Hill Associates
1535 El Paso Real
LaJolla, CA
ID:
Notes:

www.devonhillassociates.com
T:
FB:
Password:

Diversified Corporate Solutions
PO Box 278
Bridgewater, MA 02324
ID:
Notes:

www.divcorp.com
T:
FB:
Password:

Douglas Stafford
United Kingdom

ID:
Notes:

www.douglasstafford.com
T:
FB:
Password:

DSG Association Inc
2100 E 1st St, ste 106
Santa Ana, CA 92705
ID:
Notes:

www.dsgstars.com
T:
FB:
Password:

Ellis Property Mgmt Group
4324 N Beltline Rd Ste C105
Irving, TX 75038
ID:
Notes:

www.epmsonline.com
T:
FB:
Password:

Evaluation Systems for Personnel
5850 San Felipe Ste 315
Houston, TX 77057
ID:
Notes:

www.espshop.com
T:
FB:
Password:

Eyes R Us
15981 Yarnell St #215
Sylmar, CA 91342
ID:
Notes:

www.eyesrusinc.com
T:
FB:
Password:

Examine Your Practice
no address given

ID:
Notes:

www.examineyourpractice.com
T:
FB:
Password:

Excellence in Customer Service
63524 NE Pharaoh Court
Bend, OR 97701
ID:
Notes:

www.exics.com
T:
FB:
Password:

Excel Shopping & Consulting
no address given

ID:
Notes:

www.xcelshop.com
T:
FB:
Password:

Experience Exchange
(Service Intelligence)

ID:
Notes:

www.experienceexchange.com
T:
FB:
Password:

Feedback Plus Inc
5757 Alpha Road Ste 100
Dallas, TX 75240
ID:
Notes:

www.feedbackplusinc.com
T:
FB:
Password:

Focus on Service
100 Otis Street
Northborough, MA 01532
ID:
Notes:

www.focusonservice.com
T:
FB:
Password:

Franchise Compliance
PO Box 982662
Park City, UT
ID:
Notes:

www.franchisecompliance.com
T:
FB:
Password:

GAP Buster
US and worldwide

www.gapbuster.com
T:
FB:

ID:
Notes:

Password:

GfK Mystery Shopping
401 Park Ave S
New York, NY 10016
ID:
Notes:

www.cybershoppersonline.com
T:
FB:
Password:

Global Compliance
13950 Ballantyne Corp Pl Ste 300
Charlotte, NC 28277
ID:
Notes:

www.globalcompliance.com
T: tweetcompliance
FB:
Password:

Goodwin and Associates
10 Ferry Street
Concord, NH 03301
ID:
Notes:

www.mysteryshopperprogram.com
T:
FB:
Password:

Greet America Inc
3200 W. Pleasant Run Rd #400
Lancaster, TX75146
ID:
Notes:

www.greetamerica.com
T:
FB:
Password:

Graymark Security
8211 W Broward Blvd Ste 430
Ft Lauderdale, FL
ID:

www.graymarksecurity.com
T:
FB:
Password:

Notes:

The Guest Check
13386 W 22nd Place
Golden, CO 80401
ID:
Notes:

www.theguestcheck.com
T:
FB:
Password:

Harlan Clarke
no address given

ID:
Notes:

www.harlaneducation.com
T:
FB:
Password:

Hidden Concepts
US and Canada

ID:
Notes:

www.hiddenconcepts.com
T:
FB:
Password:

Hilli Dunlap Enterprises
PO Box 4597
Valley Village, CA 91615
ID:
Notes:

www.dunlapenterprises.com
T:
FB:
Password:

Hospitality Services One
1483 N. Mt Juliet Rd #223
Mt Juliet, TN 37122
ID:
Notes:

www.hsoneinc.com
T:
FB:
Password:

HR and Associates
223 Burlington Ave
Clarendon Hills, IL 60514
ID:
Notes:

www.hrandassociates.com
T:
FB:
Password:

HS Brands International
US, Europe, Asia

ID:
Notes:

www.HSbrands.com
T:
FB:
Password:

ICC/Decision Services
122 W 27th Street 10th Fl
New York, NY 10001
ID:
Notes:

www.iccds.com
T: davidjrich
FB: yes~ search their name
Password:

ICU Associates Inc
37 Birch St
Milford, MA 01757
ID:
Notes:

www.icuassociates.com
T:
FB:
Password:

Imaginus
no address given
East Amherst, NY
ID:
Notes:

www.imaginusinc.com
T:
FB:
Password:

Imyst
PO Box 7733
Ann Arbor, MI 48107
ID:
Notes:

www.imyst.com
T:
FB:
Password:

Informa
26565 Agoura Rd Ste 300
Calabasas, CA 91302
ID:
Notes:

www.informars.com
T:
FB:
Password:

Infotel
PO Box 1000
Los Gatos, CA 95124
ID:
Notes:

www.infotelinc.com
T:
FB:
Password:

Intellishop
28315 Kensington Lane Ste A
Perrysburg, OH 43551
ID:
Notes:

www.intelli-shop.com
T:
FB:
Password:

Instant Reply Inc
PO Box 11819
Ft. Lauderdale, FL 33339
ID:
Notes:

www.mysteryshopservices.com
T:
FB:
Password:

I Spy Mystery Shoppers
PO Box 45873
Omaha, NE 68145
ID:
Notes:

www.ispymysteryshoppers.com
T:
FB: yes~ search for their name
Password:

Jancyn
1912 Lincoln Ave
San Jose, CA 95159
ID:
Notes:

www.Jancyn.com
T:
FB:
Password:

JC and Associates
3578 Hartsel Drive #E-352
Colorado Springs, CO 80922
ID:
Notes:

www.jcandassociates.com
T:
FB:
Password:

JM Ridgway Company Inc.
PO Box 1050
Los Gatos, CA 95031
ID:
Notes:

www.jmridgway.com
T:
FB:
Password:

Kaiz
India

ID:
Notes:

www.kaizconsult.com
T:
FB:
Password:

Keystone
10 Holland
Irvine, CA 92618
ID:
Notes:

www.keystone2000.com
T:
FB:
Password:

Kinesis
100 W. Harrison #320
Seattle, WA 98119
ID:
Notes:

www.kinesis-cem.com
T:
FB:
Password:

LeBlanc and Associates
7040 Avenida Encinas Ste 104
Carlsbad, CA 92011
ID:
Notes:

www.mleblanc.com
T:
FB:
Password:

Management Consult Group
512 Betz Place
Metairie, LA 70005
ID:
Notes:

www.managementconsultantgroup.com
T:
FB:
Password:

Maritz Research
1355 N Highway Dr
St. Louis County, MO 63099
ID:
Notes:

www.maritzmysteryshopping.com
T:
FB:
Password:

Market Force
248 Centennial Pkwy
Louisville, CO 80027
ID:
Notes:

www.marketforce.com
T: marketforce
FB: marketforce
Password:

Marketing Systems Unlimited
1519 S. Gilbert St
Iowa City, IA 52240
ID:
Notes:

www.msultd.com
T:
FB:
Password:

Market Stat
7500 College Blvd 5th floor
Overland Park, KS 66210
ID:
Notes:

www.marketstat.com
T: marketstat
FB: yes~ search for their name
Password:

Market Viewpoint
995 Fairview Rd Ste 202
Glenmore, PA 19343
ID:
Notes:

www.marketviewpoint.com
T:
FB:
Password:

Market Wise
5601 Grande Market Dr Ste G
Appleton, WI 54913
ID:
Notes:

www.marketwi.com
T:
FB:
Password:

Mars Research
6365 NW 6th Way Ste 150
Ft Lauderdale, FL 33309
ID:
Notes:

www.marsresearch.com
T:
FB:
Password:

Mass Connections
13131 E 166th St
Cerritos, CA 90703
ID:
Notes:

www.stayingconnected.com
T:
FB: yes~ search for their name
Password:

Melinda Brody and Associates
380 S SR 434 Ste 1004
Altamonte Springs, FL 32714
ID:
Notes:

www.melindabrody.com
T: melinda407
FB: yes ~ search for their name
Password:

Mercantile Systems and Surveys
1145 2nd Street Ste A307
Brentwood, CA 94513
ID:
Notes:

www.mercsurveys.com
T:
FB:
Password:

Michelson and Associates
5232 Forest Brook Parkway
Marietta, GA 30068
ID:
Notes:

www.michelson.com
T:
FB:
Password:

Mintel International Group Ltd
213 W. Institute Pl. Ste # 208
Chicago, IL
ID:
Notes:

www.researchconsultancy.mintel.com
T: mintelnews
FB:
Password:

Mystery Guest, Inc
PO Box 3510
Winter Park, FL
ID:
Notes:

www.mysteryguestinc.com
T:
FB:
Password:

Mystery Shoppers
PO Box 50578
Knoxsville, TN 37950
ID:
Notes:

www.mystery-shoppers.com
T:
FB:
Password:

Mystique Shopper
PO Box 120921
Clermont, FL
ID:
Notes:

www.mystiqueshopper.com
T:
FB:
Password:

National Shopping Serv Net
2510 Warren Dr
Rocklin, CA 95677
ID:
Notes:

www.nationalshoppingservice.com
T: NSS_shoppers
FB: yes~ search for their name
Password:

National Shopping Service
no address given

ID:
Notes:

www.mysteryshopper.net
T:
FB:
Password:

Nationwide Services Group
10850 Pearl Rd Unit 4 D
Cleveland, OH 44136
ID:
Notes:

www.nationwidesg.com
T:
FB:
Password:

New Marketing Image
12259 New Brittany Blvd #25
Ft Meyers, FL 33907
ID:
Notes:

www.nimltd.com
T:
FB:
Password:

Nsite Mystery Shopping
4737 County Rd 101 #200
Minnetonka, MN 55345
ID:
Notes:

www.nsiteinc.com
T:
FB:
Password:

NW Loss Prevention Consultants
PO Box 3142
Renton, WA 98056
ID:
Notes:

www.nwlpc.com
T: nwlpc
FB:
Password:

Pacific Research Group
1901 Newport Blvd #350
Costa Mesa, CA 92627
ID:
Notes:

www.pacificresearchgroup.com
T:
FB:
Password:

Pat Henry
4700 Rockside Rd
Independence, OH 44131
ID:
Notes:

www.pathenry.com
T:
FB:
Password:

Patron Edge
PO Box 72
Danvers, MA 01923-0172
ID:
Notes:

www.patronedge.com
T:
FB:
Password:

Pat's Promotions
1428 E Semoran Blvd Ste 101
Apopka, FL 32703
ID:
Notes:

www.patsaim.com
T:
FB:
Password:

Perceptive Market Research
3615 SW 13th St Ste 6
Gainsville, FL 32608
ID:
Notes:

www.pmrresearch.com
T:
FB:
Password:

Performance Edge
1336 North 550 W
Pleasant Grove, UT 84062
ID:
Notes:

www.pedge.com
T:
FB:
Password:

Person to Person Quality
3919 Old Lee Hwy #81A
Alexandria, VA 22030
ID:
Notes:

www.persontopersonquality.com
T: ppquality
FB:
Password:

Pinnacle Financial Strategies
1235 N Loop W Ste 800
Houston, TX 77008
ID:
Notes:

www.pinnaclefinancialstrategies.com
T:
FB:
Password:

Promotion Network Inc
11801 SW Highway
Palo Heights, IL 60463
ID:
Notes:

www.promotionnetworkinc.com
T:
FB:
Password:

Pulse Back
PO Box 829
Manchester, VT 05254
ID:
Notes:

www.pulseback.com
T:
FB:
Password:

Quality Approach
108 Orange St Ste 4
Redlands, CA 92373
ID:
Notes:

www.qualityapproach.com
T:
FB:
Password:

Quality Assessments
PO Box 168
Rochester, IL 62563
ID:
Notes:

www.qams.com
T:
FB:
Password:

Quality Assurance Consultants
PO Box 403
Arlington, MA 02476
ID:
Notes:

www.qacinc.com
T:
FB:
Password:

Quality Marketing Inc
PO Box 746
High Point, NC 27261
ID:
Notes:

www.quality-marketing.com
T:
FB:
Password:

Quality Works Associates
PO Box 35341
Brighton, MA 02135
ID:
Notes:

www.qualityworks.com
T:
FB:
Password:

Quest for the Best
PO Box 280933
Memphis, TN 38168
ID:
Notes:

www.questforbest.com
T:
FB:
Password:

Reality Based Group
no address given

ID:
Notes:

www.mysteryshopinc.com
T:
FB:
Password:

Reality Check
11539 24th Ave NE
Seattle, WA
ID:
Notes:

www.rcmysteryshopper.com
T:
FB:
Password:

Rentrak
North America, Europe
South America
ID:
Notes:

www.ms.rentrak.com
T:
FB:
Password:

Restaurant Cops
511 Lasso Loop
Canyon Lake, TX 78133
ID:
Notes:

www.restaurant-cops.com
T:
FB:
Password:

Restaurant Evaluators
500 N Michigan Ave
Chicago, IL
ID:
Notes:

www.restaurantevaluators.com
T:
FB:
Password:

Retail Eyes
1501 N Sepulveda Blvd
Manhattan Beach, CA 90266
ID:
Notes:

www.retaileyes.com
T:
FB:
Password:

Retail Track
300 Earl Grey Dr Ste 370
Kanata, ONT K2T 1C1
ID:
Notes:

www.retailtrack.com
T:
FB:
Password:

Rickie Kruh Research
4907 Midtown lane Ste 1210
Palm Beach Gardens, FL 33418
ID:
Notes:

www.rkrmg.com
T:
FB:
Password:

Ritter and Assoc
209 N Reynolds Rd
Toledo, OH 43615
ID:
Notes:

www.Ritterandassociates.com
T:
FB:
Password:

RGIS Inventory Specialists
US, Canada, Europe, Asia
South America
ID:
Notes:

www.rgisinv.com
T:
FB:
Password:

Rocky Mountain Merchandising
1736 E. Holladay Rd
Salt Lake City, UT 84124
ID:
Notes:

www.rockymm.com
T:
FB:
Password:

Satisfaction Services
PO Box 11045
Ft Lauderdale, FL 33301
ID:
Notes:

www.satisfactionservicesinc.com
T:
FB:
Password:

Second to None
3045 Miller Road
Ann Arbor, MI 48103
ID:
Notes:

www.second-to-none.com
T:
FB:
Password:

Secret Shoppers
620 Mendelssohn Ave N
Minneapolis, MN 55427
ID:
Notes:

www.secretshopper.com
T:
FB:
Password:

Secret Shopping Services
12414 158th St
Puyllaup, WA 98374
ID:
Notes:

www.secretshoppingservices.com
T:
FB:
Password:

Sensors Quality Management
895 Don Mills St Ste 400
Toronto, ONT CAN M3C 1W3
ID:
Notes:

www.sqm.ca
T:
FB:
Password:

Service Alliance
14826 E Caspian Place
Aurora, CO 80014
ID:
Notes:

www.servicealliance inc.com
T:
FB:
Password:

Service Check
167 C. Central Ave
Pacific Grove, CA 93950
ID:
Notes:

www.servicecheck.com
T:
FB:
Password:

Service Evaluation Concepts
210 Crossways Pk Dr
Woodbury, NY 11797
ID:
Notes:

www.serviceevaluation.com
T:
FB:
Password:

Service Excellence Group
15323 Laude Farm Rd
St. Louis, MO 63141
ID:
Notes:

www.serviceexcellencegroup.com
T:
FB:
Password:

Service Impressions
9316 Nestani Way
Elk Grove, CA 95758
ID:
Notes:

www.serviceimpressions.com
T:
FB:
Password:

Service Performance Group
307 S. Salem Street Ste 201
Apex, NC 27502
ID:
Notes:

www.spgweb.com
T:
FB:
Password:

Service Quality Department
1063 Todos Santos Station
Concord, CA 94522
ID:
Notes:

www.service-quality.com
T:
FB:
Password:

Service Research Corp
601 Old Cheney Rd Ste C
Lincoln, NE 68512
ID:
Notes:

www.serviceresearch.com
T:
FB:
Password:

Service Savvy
16312 50th Ave N
Plymouth, MN 55446
ID:
Notes:

www.servicesavvy.com
T:
FB:
Password:

Service Sense
PO Box 650
Nowell, MA
ID:
Notes:

www.servicesense.com
T:
FB:
Password:

Service TRAC
9188 E San Salvador Drive
Scottsdale, AZ 85258
ID:
Notes:

www.servicetrac.com
T:
FB:
Password:

Shadow Agency
5520 Davis Blvd
North Richland Hills, TX 76180
ID:
Notes:

www.theshadowagency.com
T:
FB:
Password:

Shadow Shopper of GA
PO Box 3357
Cumming, GA 30028
ID:
Notes:

www.tssog.com
T:
FB:
Password:

Shop Talk Service Evaluations
PO Box 1543
Bothell, WA 98011
ID:
Notes:

www.shoptalkservice.com
T:
FB:
Password:

Shoppers Critique
1969 Corporate Square
Longwood, FL 32750
ID:
Notes:

www.shopperscritique.com
T: shopsalert
FB: yes~ search for their name
Password:

Shoppers Inc
PO Box 2912
Broken Arrow, OK 74012
ID:
Notes:

www.shopperjobs.com
T:
FB: yes~ search for their name
Password:

Shopper's View
1331Plainfield Ave NE
Grand Rapids, MI 49505
ID:
Notes:

www.shoppersview.com
T:
FB:
Password:

Sinclair Service Assessment
900 ISOM Rd Ste 110
San Antonio, TX 78216
ID:
Notes:

www.sinclaircustomermetrics.com
T:
FB:
Password:

SkilCheck Services
651 N Cherokee Lane Ste A
Lodi, CA 95240
ID:
Notes:

www.skilcheck.com
T:
FB:
Password:

The Solomon Group
12463 Rancho Bernardo Rd #149
San Diego, CA
ID:
Notes:

www.thesolomongroup.com
T:
FB:
Password:

Spies In Disguise
PO Box 14167
Grand Rapids, MI
ID:
Notes:

www.spiesindisguise.com
T:
FB:
Password:

Spot Check Services
1540 Albert Street
Regina SK CAN S4P 2S4
ID:
Notes:

www.spotcheckservices.com
T:
FB:
Password:

Strategic Reflections
4424 Alcholtz Rd Ste C-3
Cincinnati, OH 45245
ID:
Notes:

www.strategicreflections.com
T:
FB:
Password:

Test Shopper
California

ID:
Notes:

www.testshopper.com
T:
FB:
Password:

Texas Shopper Network
908 Town and Country Blvd Ste 120
Houston, TX 77024
ID:
Notes:

www.texasshoppersnetwork.com
T:
FB:
Password:

Trendsource Inc
4891 Pacific Hwy ste 200
San Diego, CA 92110
ID:
Notes:

www.trendsource.com
F:
TB:
Password:

Verites
3500 W. Olive Ave Ste 700
Burbank, CA 91505
ID:
Notes:

www.tnsmi-tes.com
T:
FB:
Password:

Scheduler Listings

These scheduling companies work with several mystery shopping companies at once to help schedule assignments to mystery shoppers. The benefit to signing on with them is that you'll be considered for shops from "ABC mystery shopping company" and "XYZ mystery shopping company" and everyone in between. Make sure you sign on with scheduling companies IN ADDITION to mystery shopping companies!

Coast to Coast Scheduling
15903 Lawnhill Dr
Li Mirada, CA

www.ctcss.com
T: ctcsservices
FB: yes~ search for their name

ID:

Password:

Notes:

Hunts Home Network
no address available
Dallas, TX

www.dawnhuntsdatabase.com
T:
FB:

ID:

Password:

Notes:

Kern Scheduling Services
PO Box 14094
Tuscon, AZ

www.kernscheduling.com
T: kssinc
FB: yes~ search for their name

ID: Password:

Notes:

Palm Scheduling Services **www.palmschedulingservices.com**
13153 Michelle Circle
Whittier, CA
T:
FB:

ID: Password:

Notes:

Quality Scheduling Group **www.qualityscheduling.com**
no address available
New Jersey
T:
FB:

ID: Password:

Notes:

Professional Organizations

As with any industry there are professional "guilds" in mystery shopping. The organizations listed below have mystery shopping Companies and Merchandising companies as members. While these companies are *not for shoppers* to sign on with, some offer resources, like training, education, conventions, and job boards. You can browse their sites to learn more about what it's like from the company's point of view to set up a mystery shopping program, or just make sure that a company is legitimate.

World Association of Opinion and Market Research Professionals (ESOMAR)
Vondelstraat 172
1054 GV Amsterdam
The Netherlands
www.esomar.org

From their website: "ESOMAR is the world's leading market research association and is recognised as the premier international industry advocate… it (is) the only organisation that unites market research professionals on a worldwide level." You can use this resource to find companies that do international mystery shopping.

International Mystery Shopping Alliance (IMSA)
North America Division:
210 Crossways park Drive

Woodbury, NY 11797
www.theimsa.com

From their website: "IMSA offers the one-stop solution for all organisations needing global or local mystery shopping services and related services." This organization is geared towards companies, not shoppers, which operate on an international scale. You can use this resource to find companies that do international mystery shopping.

Market Research Association (MRA)
PO Box 230
1344 Silas Dean Hwy #306
Rocky Hill, CT 06067
www.mra-net.org

From their website: "To protect the marketing research environment, we will act as an advocate with appropriate government entities, other associations, and the public. MRA is a key source for assistance and training information. It is where researchers learn of new opportunities, markets and potential obstacles to future success." You can use this resource to learn more about the Market Research Industry.

Mystery Shopping Providers Association (MSPA)
2695 Villa Creek Dr #260
Dallas, TX 75234
www.mysteryshop.org

From their website: "The MSPA is the largest professional trade association dedicated to improving service quality using anonymous resources. With over 150 member companies worldwide, our diverse membership includes marketing research and merchandising companies, private investigation firms, training organizations and companies that specialize in providing mystery shopping services. Our member companies work with their clients to establish mechanisms to measure and improve levels of service."

The MSPA is *the* resource for finding job postings and reputable companies to work with. You can find assignments by location, and there are forums to post information and questions as well. The MSPA also offer a silver certification course for $15, and a $99 gold certification course, which is highly regarded in the industry.

National Association for Retail Merchandising Services(NARMS)
PO Box 906
Plover, WI 54467
www.narms.com

From their website: "NARMS drives, promotes, expands, and fosters the business of providing retail merchandising and marketing and sales marketing services to all classes of trade by providing the merchandising and marketing industry with quality research, strong educational programs and better networking opportunities." Use NARMS to find job listings and post a profile for free. They have training courses available too.

National Coalition For Professional Mystery Shoppers and Merchandisers (NCPMS)
PO Box 311573
Tampa, FL 33680
www.justshop.org

From their website: "The National Center for Professional Mystery Shoppers and Merchandisers is a not-for-profit organization that strives to educate and empower the diverse online population of mystery shopping and merchandising professionals by providing Internet based support." You can use this resource for their message boards, certification courses, and training.

Web Forums/More Info

Mystery Shoppers mainly work alone. We don't really have a water cooler to hang out around and kvetch about the boss. But, we do have web forums! Log onto these forums to find out what your fellow mystery shoppers are saying about assignments, companies, and other shopping adventures!

Shopper Support and Job Listings

The BEST place to find job listings is **www.JobSlinger.com**

The oldest mystery shopper forum: **volition.com/mystery.html**
You can ask question, get feedback on companies and find assignments.

The MSPA site: **www.mysteryshop.org**
They have a forum, job postings, and a list of member companies.

And there are a few others to choose from:

www.shoppersupport.com

www.mysteryshopresources.com

Assignment Services

If you are looking to get more assignments, you can always sign up with a database system, where companies and schedulers go to recruit shoppers and fill assignments.

Hire A Shopper: **www.hireashopper.com** lists of companies assignments delivered to your e-mail directly, and you can search companies in a given area. $25/year.

Mystery Shopping Solutions: **www.mystshopsol.com,** member MSPA, sign up on their site to have your information viewed by mystery shopping companies, there is a fee involved.

Select A Shopper: **www.selectashopper.com** list your info, and it will be distributed to companies 4 times a year. $25/year.

Shadow Shopper: **www.shadowshopper.com** assignments delivered to your e-mail as they are available. $0-$29/year

Scam Alert!

Below is a listing of web links that will give you a good indication of the scams that are out there. Remember, you should NEVER have to pay to be listed with a company, you should NEVER give out your bank account number to do a bank shop, and you have NO NEED to ever pay for any more information. There is more than enough to get you started within this book.

www.michelson.com/aboutus/article2.html

www.sohojobs.org/scam2.html

www.mysteryshoppercoach.com/mysteryshopperscams.html

You can also visit my website: **www.QueenoftheRandomJob.com** for various mystery shopping, Work at Home, Random Job, and Scam information, or read *I Got Scammed, So You Don't Have To!* for tips on how to spot scammers and find legitimate work.

Blank Forms

Sample Retail Evaluation

Store name: ____________________ Date: ____________________
Store Address: ____
Time Entered: ____________________ Time Left: ____________________
Associate's name/description: ______________________________
Shopper's description: _____________________________________

INITIAL IMPRESSIONS

Was the exterior of the store clean?	YES ☐	NO ☐
Was the parking lot well lit?	YES ☐	NO ☐
Was the store adequately lit?	YES ☐	NO ☐
Was the overall condition good?	YES ☐	NO ☐
Was the music at an appropriate level?	YES ☐	NO ☐
Was the merchandise well stocked?	YES ☐	NO ☐
Did the merchandise have price tags?	YES ☐	NO ☐
Were signs legible?	YES ☐	NO ☐
Was the floor clean?	YES ☐	NO ☐

COMMENTS: ____
____
____

GREETING

Was your greeting prompt? YES ☐ NO ☐
Time it took to be greeted: ____________
Were you greeted in a friendly manner? YES ☐ NO ☐
Exact Greeting: ______________________________
Were there enough salespeople for the amount of traffic in the store?
YES ☐ NO ☐

COMMENTS: ____
____
____

PRODUCT PRESENTATION
ITEM REQUESTED: ______________________________

Sample Retail Evaluation continued

Did the associate determine your needs? YES ☐ NO ☐
Did they suggest an appropriate item? YES ☐ NO ☐
Item suggested: ____________________
Did they know where the item was located? YES ☐ NO ☐
Did the associate inform you of the benefits? YES ☐ NO ☐
Did the associate answer your questions? YES ☐ NO ☐
If the associate couldn't answer your questions, did they refer you to someone who could? YES ☐ NO ☐
Name and description of associate: ____________________

Did the associate overcome your objection? YES ☐ NO ☐
Objection used, and the associate's response: ____________________

____
Did the associate offer other merchandise complimentary to their initial suggestion? YES ☐ NO ☐
Item suggested: ____________________

COMMENTS: ____________________

____

____

COMMON COURTESIES
Was the associate:

Courteous?	YES ☐	NO ☐
Respectful?	YES ☐	NO ☐
Helpful?	YES ☐	NO ☐
Efficient?	YES ☐	NO ☐
Knowledgeable?	YES ☐	NO ☐
Did you feel that the associate wanted to help you?	YES ☐	NO ☐
Based on your experience, would you return?	YES ☐	NO ☐

COMMENTS: ____________________

____

____

Sample Retail Evaluation continued

Please tell us about your experience from beginning to end:

Sample Financial Evaluation

Branch: ______________________ Date: ____________
Branch Address: ____________________ Time entered: _________
Employee's Name or Description: _____________________________
Shopper's Description: _____________________________________

AT FIRST GLANCE

Was the exterior of the branch clean? YES ☐ NO ☐
Was the parking lot well maintained? YES ☐ NO ☐
Were there adequate envelopes at the ATM? YES ☐ NO ☐
Was the interior clean? YES ☐ NO ☐
How many customers were waiting in the teller line? __________
How many windows were open? ____________
Were sufficient transaction slips available? YES ☐ NO ☐
How many people were at the new accounts counter? ___________
Were there posters or displays of promotions or products?
YES ☐ NO ☐

COMMENTS: ____
____
____
____

GREETING

Was your greeting/acknowledgment prompt? YES ☐ NO ☐
Time it took to be greeted:_________________
Were you greeted in a friendly manner? YES ☐ NO ☐
Exact Greeting: ________________________________

COMMENTS: ____
____
____
____

QUALIFYING

SERVICE REQUESTED: ________________________________

Sample Financial Evaluation continued

Did the associate determine:

Your name?	YES ☐	NO ☐
Your contact information?	YES ☐	NO ☐
Your profession?	YES ☐	NO ☐
Where you currently bank?	YES ☐	NO ☐
The amount of funds you usually kept in your accounts?	YES ☐	NO ☐
Your purposes for the accounts?	YES ☐	NO ☐

COMMENTS: ____

____

____

____

PRESENTATION

Did the associate offer a suitable service?	YES ☐	NO ☐
Was the associate discreet?	YES ☐	NO ☐
Did the associate offer other products?	YES ☐	NO ☐
If so, what else was offered? ______________________		
Did the associate seem interested in helping you?	YES ☐	NO ☐
Did the associate mention specific account information?	YES ☐	NO ☐

(Please note any specifics in the comment section)

COMMENTS: ____

____

____

____

CLOSE

Did the associate offer to set up an account today?	YES ☐	NO ☐
Did the associate overcome your objection?	YES ☐	NO ☐
What was your objection? ______________________		
Did the associate offer a business card or brochure?	YES ☐	NO ☐

What reason did you give for not opening an account today? ______________

____

Sample Financial Evaluation continued

How did the associate respond? ________________________________

____

COMMENTS: ____

____

____

ATTITUDE

Was the associate:

Pleasant?	YES ☐ NO ☐
Courteous?	YES ☐ NO ☐
Respectful?	YES ☐ NO ☐
Attentive?	YES ☐ NO ☐
Was the employee genuinely interested in your business?	YES ☐ NO ☐
Would you have opened an account based on this experience?	YES ☐ NO ☐

Please answer why or why not: __________________________________

____

If the associate could not help you, were you referred ? YES ☐ NO ☐

To whom? ____

COMMENTS: ____

____

____

PLEASE COMMENT ON YOUR EXPERIENCE

____

____

____

____

____

____

____

____

Sample Restaurant Evaluation

Date: ____________	Day and Time: ________________
Location: ____________________	Server: ______________________
Address: ____________________________________	
Number in party:_______ Total Score: _______________________	
Service Score: ________________	Location Score: _______________

PLEASE SCORE FROM 1-5 WITH 5 BEING THE BEST

INITIAL IMPRESSIONS (please rate 1-5)

__ Did the restaurant make a welcoming impression from the street?

__ Was the exterior of the restaurant clean?

__ Was the parking lot well lit?

__ Did the landscaping look well-maintained?

COMMENTS: ____

____

____

ATMOSPHERE (please rate 1-5)

__Was the music at an appropriate level?

__Were the staff dressed in uniform?

__Was lighting at an appropriate level?

__Was the interior of the restaurant inviting?

__Were the aisles easy to maneuver around?

__Were restroom signs clearly noted?

COMMENTS: ____

____

____

HOST STAND (please rate 1-5)

Host Name: ______________ Time Entered: _____________

__How many guests were in line to be seated?

__Were you put on a waiting list?

Sample Restaurant Evaluation continued

__Did the host greet you in a friendly manner?
__Was the host appropriately dressed?
__Did the host determine your seating preference?
__If an estimate time was given, was it met?

COMMENTS: ____
____
____

AT THE TABLE (please rate 1-5)
Server: __________ Time Sat: _________ Time Greeted: ___________
__Was the table set with the appropriate amount of flatware?
__Were the salt and pepper shakers filled?
__Did the server greet you in a friendly manner?
__Did the server offer you his/her name?
__Did the server offer you something from the bar?
__Did the server check for photo ID, (if under 35)
Bar items ordered:________________________________
____

ORDERING (please rate 1-5)
___Did the server offer appetizers?
___Were the daily specials noted?
___Was the server able to answer questions you had about the entrees?
Entrees ordered: ________________________________

COMMENTS: ____
____
____

DELIVERY OF FOOD (please rate 1-5)
TIME ORDER RECEIVED: _____________
____Did you receive what you had ordered?
____Was the presentation of the food favorable?

Sample Restaurant Evaluation continued

____Was the food tasteful?
____Did the server offer complimentary items?
____Did the server offer to refill beverages?

COMMENTS: ____
____
____

FOLLOW UP (please rate 1-5)
TIME SERVER CHECKED BACK: __________
___Did the server offer dessert?
Time it took to receive dessert: __________________________
___Did the server offer after dinner drinks?
Time it took to receive after dinner drinks: ________________________
___Did the server or busser clear empty plates?

COMMENTS: ____
____
____

RECEIVING THE BILL (please rate 1-5)
TIME SERVER DROPPED OFF BILL: __________
____Did the bill have the correct amount charged?
____Did the server leave any promotional items (i.e., mints) with the bill?

COMMENTS: ____
____
____

TIME RECEIPT WAS RECEIVED: __________

Sample Restaurant Evaluation continued

PLEASE RATE OUR MANNER (please rate 1-5)

	Your Host	Your Server	Other Staff
Friendliness			
Helpfulness			
Sincerity			
Courtesy			
Knowledge			
Enthusiasm			

Please note the other staff you came in contact with: ____________________
Based on your experience, would you return? ____________________

Why or why not? ____

____

____

PLEASE RATE OUR DINING ROOM (please rate 1-5)

	Dining Room	Bar/Lounge	Restroom
Floors			
Seats/Stalls			
Tables/Counters			
Courtesy			
Supplies			

PLEASE COMMENT ON YOUR EXPERIENCE

____

____

____

____

____

____

____

Sample Real Estate Evaluation

Property: ____________________ Leasing Agent: ____________________
Date:______________ Day: ______________ Shopper ID: ______________

COVER STORY Size apartment desired: ______________
Date moving: ______________ Employer: ______________
Currently live: ____________________ Number of residents: ______________
Reason for Moving: ____
Advertising Source Used: ____

TELEPHONE CONSULTATION
Property: ___________________________ Leasing Agent____________________
Date of Call: ______________ Time of Call: ______________

____How many attempts did it take to reach your target/leasing agent?
Describe your attempts to reach the office and your target: ______________

PLEASE TELL US ABOUT THE GREETING
How many rings to answer the phone? ______________
Were you placed on hold? ______________ For how long? ___________
Did the agent have a memorable greeting? YES ☐ NO ☐
What was the agent's greeting? ____________________________
Did the agent state the name of the property? YES ☐ NO ☐
Did the agent offer his/her name? YES ☐ NO ☐
Did the agent ask for your name? YES ☐ NO ☐

COMMENTS: ____
____
____

PLEASE TELL US ABOUT THE QUALIFICATION PROCESS
Did the agent...
Ask when you needed an apartment? YES ☐ NO ☐
Ask the size you needed? YES ☐ NO ☐

Sample Real Estate Evaluation continued

Ask your price range?	YES ☐	NO ☐
Ask the number of residents?	YES ☐	NO ☐
Ask about pets?	YES ☐	NO ☐
Identify your specific needs?	YES ☐	NO ☐
Ask about your work?	YES ☐	NO ☐
Ask about the ad source?	YES ☐	NO ☐
Ask why you were moving?	YES ☐	NO ☐

If your needs couldn't be met, were you referred to another community?
YES ☐ N/A ☐ NO ☐

COMMENTS: ____

____

____

PLEASE TELL US ABOUT THE AGENT'S PRESENTATION

Did the agent…

Describe the features of the apartment?	YES ☐	NO ☐
Offer the square footage?	YES ☐	NO ☐
Describe the features of the community?	YES ☐	NO ☐
Describe the area conveniences?	YES ☐	NO ☐
Offer the price?	YES ☐	NO ☐
Offer a promotion or incentive to visit?	YES ☐	NO ☐

Incentive offered: _______________________________

COMMENTS: ____

____

____

PLEASE TELL US ABOUT THE CLOSE

Did the agent…

Ask you to visit the property?	YES ☐	NO ☐
Offer an appointment time?	YES ☐	NO ☐
Offer clear directions?	YES ☐	NO ☐
Ask for your contact information?	YES ☐	NO ☐
Thank you for calling?	YES ☐	NO ☐

Sample Real Estate Evaluation continued

COMMENTS: ____

____

____

PLEASE TELL US ABOUT THE AGENT'S MANNER

Did the agent...

Have a good control over the conversation?	YES ☐	NO ☐
Seem natural on the phone?	YES ☐	NO ☐
Direct the call to your interests?	YES ☐	NO ☐
Create a sense of urgency to visit the property?	YES ☐	NO ☐

Did you feel like the agent was interested in showing you the apartment?

YES ☐ NO ☐

COMMENTS: ____

____

____

ON SITE EVALUATION

Property: ______________________ Leasing Agent: ____________

Date: ____________ Day: ____________ Arrival Time: ____________

PLEASE TELL US ABOUT YOUR INITIAL IMPRESSIONS

Did you easily find the community?	YES ☐	NO ☐
Were signs visible to the community and leasing office?	YES ☐	NO ☐
Were signs/banners in good condition?	YES ☐	NO ☐
Were the buildings in good condition?	YES ☐	NO ☐
Was the parking lot clear and free of debris?	YES ☐	NO ☐
Was the landscaping in good condition?	YES ☐	NO ☐
Was your first impression of the community good?	YES ☐	NO ☐

COMMENTS: ____

____

____

Sample Real Estate Evaluation continued

PROPERTY EVALUATION

PLEASE TELL US ABOUT THE OFFICE CONDITION

Was the office open, clean and ready for business?	YES ☐	NO ☐
Was the office desk area neat and organized?	YES ☐	NO ☐
Were the Fair Housing/Rental Requirements posted?	YES ☐	NO ☐

COMMENTS: ____

____

____

WERE THE APARTMENT FEATURES IN GOOD CONDITION?

Walls and paint	YES ☐	NO ☐
Carpeting	YES ☐	NO ☐
Windows/blinds	YES ☐	NO ☐
Bathroom: floor, toilet, sink, mirror, cabinets	YES ☐	NO ☐
Kitchen: floor, sink, cabinets, appliances	YES ☐	NO ☐
Closets	YES ☐	NO ☐
Lights	YES ☐	NO ☐
Balcony	YES ☐	NO ☐
Stairs, interior and/or exterior	YES ☐	NO ☐

COMMENTS: ____

____

PLEASE TELL US ABOUT THE PROPERTY CONDITION

List amenities available and whether you viewed them

Clubhouse	YES ☐	NO ☐	VIEWED ☐
Pool/Jacuzzi	YES ☐	NO ☐	VIEWED ☐
Sauna	YES ☐	NO ☐	VIEWED ☐
Exercise room	YES ☐	NO ☐	VIEWED ☐
Office Center	YES ☐	NO ☐	VIEWED ☐
Outdoor tennis/basketball courts	YES ☐	NO ☐	VIEWED ☐
Racquetball courts	YES ☐	NO ☐	VIEWED ☐
Laundry Room	YES ☐	NO ☐	VIEWED ☐

Sample Real Estate Evaluation continued

Other: ______________________________

Did the property give a favorable impression overall? YES ☐ NO ☐

COMMENTS: ______________________________

____

____

PLEASE TELL US ABOUT YOUR ONSITE GREETING

Did the agent…

Acknowledge you promptly?	YES ☐	NO ☐
Smile and stand to greet you?	YES ☐	NO ☐
Introduce him or herself?	YES ☐	NO ☐
Offer you a seat or refreshments?	YES ☐	NO ☐
Remember your phone call?	YES ☐	NO ☐
Shake your hand and ask your name?	YES ☐	NO ☐
Use your name throughout the tour?	YES ☐	NO ☐

COMMENTS: ______________________________

____

____

PLEASE TELL US ABOUT YOUR ONSITE QUALIFICATION

Did the Associate use a welcome card, ask you to fill out a welcome card, or ask:

a) date desired	YES ☐	NO ☐
b) size needed	YES ☐	NO ☐
c) number of occupants	YES ☐	NO ☐
d) if you had pets	YES ☐	NO ☐
e) where you were working	YES ☐	NO ☐
f) where you were living	YES ☐	NO ☐

Sample Real Estate Evaluation continued

g) why you were moving YES ☐ NO ☐
h) your contact information YES ☐ NO ☐
Did the agent ask for any special needs? YES ☐ NO ☐

COMMENTS: ______________________________
____
____

PLEASE TELL US ABOUT THE PRE-TOUR
Did the Agent…
Show you floor plans? YES ☐ NO ☐
Show you the apartment on the community map? YES ☐ NO ☐
If no vacancies were available for showing, did the agent:
a) show you floor plans? YES ☐ NO ☐ N/A ☐
b) show you a model? YES ☐ NO ☐ N/A ☐
c) show you an occupied apartment? YES ☐ NO ☐ N/A ☐
d) offer another appointment? YES ☐ NO ☐ N/A ☐

Did the agent ask for I.D. before the tour? YES ☐ NO ☐
COMMENTS: ______________________________
____
____

PLEASE TELL US ABOUT THE AGENT'S DEMONSTRATION
Did you see a model, vacant apartment, neither, or both?
M ☐ **V** ☐ **N** ☐ **B** ☐
Please list the number of the apartment(s) shown: __________

Did the agent…
Have a good control over the conversation? YES ☐ NO ☐
Mention onsite staff YES ☐ NO ☐
Discuss the property benefits / amenities? YES ☐ NO ☐

Sample Real Estate Evaluation continued

Show all recreation areas?	YES ☐	NO ☐
Discuss the area benefits?	YES ☐	NO ☐
Demonstrate the features and benefits?	YES ☐	NO ☐
Increase the value (parking included, paid utilities)	YES ☐	NO ☐
Use your name throughout the tour?	YES ☐	NO ☐
Was the agent rushed or hurried?	YES ☐	NO ☐

COMMENTS: ____

____

____

PLEASE TELL US ABOUT YOUR OBJECTIONS AND THE CLOSE

Did the agent…

Ask closing questions throughout tour?	YES ☐	NO ☐
Create a sense of urgency	YES ☐	NO ☐
Attempt to overcome your objections?	YES ☐	NO ☐

What was your objection, and how did the agent overcome it?

____

____

Seem comfortable with the price?	YES ☐	NO ☐
Explain any move-in costs and fees?	YES ☐	NO ☐
Did the agent attempt a close?	YES ☐	NO ☐
Did the agent attempt a second close?	YES ☐	NO ☐
How did the agent ask you to commit?		
a) by filling out an application	YES ☐	NO ☐
b) by leaving a deposit	YES ☐	NO ☐
c) by leaving a hold	YES ☐	NO ☐
e) by renting the apartment	YES ☐	NO ☐
f) the agent didn't ask for a commitment	YES ☐	NO ☐
Did the agent offer incentives or promotions?	YES ☐	NO ☐

What incentives did the agent offer? ______________________

How did the agent react to you not renting the apartment? __________

____

Sample Real Estate Evaluation continued

COMMENTS: ____
____
____

PLEASE TELL US ABOUT THE AGENT'S ATTITUDE AND APPEARANCE

Was the agent enthusiastic, genuine, and attentive?	YES ☐	NO ☐
Was the agent's presentation natural, not rehearsed?	YES ☐	NO ☐
Did the agent establish a rapport with you?	YES ☐	NO ☐
Was the agent dressed appropriately?	YES ☐	NO ☐
Did the agent display a professional attitude?	YES ☐	NO ☐

COMMENTS: ____
____
____

PLEASE TELL US ABOUT YOUR OVERALL EXPERIENCE
____
____
____
____
____
____
____
____
____
____
____
____
____
____
____
____

About the Author

At some point in her life, Bethany has worked as a puppeteer, dog walker, art gallery owner, waitress, child-care provider, book/music seller, actor, sexual health resource clinic advisor, model, baseball score-keeper, customer-service evaluator, merchandiser, mystery shopping company owner, elderly care giver, phone book deliverer, hotel brochure canvasser, pre-school teacher, artist, music and performance venue coordinator, web designer and coder, community education teacher, census taker, election worker, Internet business owner, virtual assistant, standardized test scorer, Pilates studio manager, housekeeper for Bill Gates and Paul Allen, landlord and property manager, vacuum salesman, surveyor, tutor, marketer, project innovator, writer, small business consultant and revenue-generator, and of course, Ronald McDonald's bodyguard.

All of these fabulous (and not so fabulous) experiences have led her to being dubbed, "Queen of the Random Job." After all, she needed ways to supplement her puppetry habit but still find ways to eat!

After over 10 years of trial and error, she has finally found ways to share all of her hard-learned lessons and help others identify scams and find legitimate work. Bethany has created books, training programs, websites and resources to assist others on finding ways to make ends meet and still live their avant-garde passions. Bethany is available for online and in-person workshops and consultations.

Bethany Mooradian

"Queen Buzzy"

www.QueenoftheRandomJob.com

www.QueenBuzzy.com/twitter

www.QueenBuzzy.com/facebook

Also by Bethany Mooradian

I Got Scammed So You Don't Have To!

www.avoidjobscams.com

There is nothing worse than sitting down with your checkbook at the end of the month and realizing that you don't have enough to meet your basic needs. It's happening a lot right now: unemployment is running rampant, people are getting laid off in massive numbers, savings and investments are drying up quickly, and many people are relying on their credit cards to cover basic necessities.

Having an extra job, or other random sources of income, could mean the difference between constant worry and financial stability. But what do you do when you can't distinguish between legitimate work and a clever ploy?

Bethany Mooradian, Queen of the Random Job, offers over 300 ideas, resources, and legitimate companies that can help you bridge the income gap. Using her experience and knowledge in Internet marketing, she reveals the most common tricks of scammers. She empowers you with the resources to research companies and job offers so you'll never have to ask, "Is this job for real?"

I Got Scammed, So You Don't Have To! offers a ton of valuable information:

Techniques of Scammers and Common Scams: A behind-the-scenes look at Internet marketing essential for anyone who uses the Web and e-mail.

Making Money: Over 170 companies, ideas, and resources to create your own business or side income from your talents, skills, and assets.

Get a Random Job: Over 140 legitimate companies that offer flexible work environments, or hire at-home-workers.

Creating a Business: We can no longer trust our employers to take care of us! Now non-entrepreneurs can develop a new mindset and open their hearts to the joy of small business ownership.

Also from Moreradiant Publishing

The Repatriate

www.TheRepatriate.com

In the early months of 1947, eighteen-year-old Tom Mooradian had everything -- Hollywood good looks, high academic ranking in his senior class at Southwestern High School, recognition by the three Detroit daily newspapers as being one of the finest basketball talents in the Public School League and in the state. Before the end of that year, however, he would find himself with hundreds of other Soviet citizens, standing in long unruly lines hoping to purchase a kilo of black, damp, sawdust filled bread. He was fighting the daily fight for survival in the Soviet Union.

But bread was the least of his worries; he was not allowed to travel or utter one word against the state in public or private conversation. Mooradian had lost his freedom. It was not a dream, but a nightmare that he and 150 other American Armenians willingly, but unknowingly, walked into when they signed up for the Armenian Repatriation.

Shortly after their arrival in Erevan, the NKVD, (the Soviet Secret Police) arrested Mooradian as he boarded a plane for Moscow. Beaten at the airport, Mooradian was conveyed to NKVD headquarters, his crime: he had authored and agreed to present a petition, he and three other repatriates had signed, to the US Ambassador, pleading for help to return to the United States.

Mooradian's basketball prowess captured the hearts of the Soviet people and saved his life. Miraculously surviving 13 years behind the Iron Curtain, he had the opportunity to see what no foreign correspondent, no western journalist, no diplomat was permitted to see: the Soviet Union as the Soviets lived.

Filled with political drama, romance, and intrigue, Tom's autobiography, *The Repatriate* reads like a novel, and will have you guessing how Tom managed to return to America alive.

TRIBEStrack

Comprehensive Scheduling and Accounting System

www.TRIBEStrack.com

As an independent contractor, sometimes we spend just as much, if not more time on keeping track of our business as we do actually completing our assignments!

TRIBEStrack is a unique system that takes care of the nitty-gritty details so you can focus on completing your work. Combining both scheduling and accounting software it is an all-in-one solution for the Entrepreneur, Solopreneur or Independent Contractor. You'll be able to:

- Create comprehensive company profiles with contact information
- Log any specifics about assignments, schedulers, or companies
- Schedule assignments, appointments, or work to complete
- Keep track of deductions, expenses and mileage
- Run reports to see income from specific companies, assignments, or over a certain time frame
- And more!

Get rid of your filing system, your spreadsheets, and discover how TRIBEStrack can make your business more efficient!

Learn more at **www.TRIBEStrack.com**